The Wars of
the Roses

Titles in the World History Series

WORLD HISTORY SERIES ■ ■ ■

The Wars of the Roses

by
William W. Lace

Lucent Books, P.O. Box 289011, San Diego, CA 92198-9011

Library of Congress Cataloging-in-Publication Data

Lace, William W.
　　The Wars of the Roses / by William W. Lace.
　　　　p.　cm.—(World history series)
　　Includes bibliographical references and index.
　　ISBN 1-56006-419-6　(lib. ed.: alk. paper)
　　1. Great Britain—History—Wars of the Roses, 1455–1485—
Juvenile literature.　[1. Great Britain—History—Wars of the
Roses, 1455–1485.]　　I.Title. II. Series.
　　DA250.L24　　1996
　　942.04—dc20　　　　　　　　　　　　　　　　　　95-14367
　　　　　　　　　　　　　　　　　　　　　　　　　　　　　CIP
　　　　　　　　　　　　　　　　　　　　　　　　　　　　　AC

Copyright 1996 by Lucent Books, Inc., P.O. Box 289011,
San Diego, California 92198-9011

Printed in the U.S.A.

Contents

1000425980/

Foreword

Each year on the first day of school, nearly every history teacher faces the task of explaining why his or her students should study history. One logical answer to this question is that exploring what happened in our past explains how the things we often take for granted—our customs, ideas, and institutions—came to be. As statesman and historian Winston Churchill put it, "Every nation or group of nations has its own tale to tell. Knowledge of the trials and struggles is necessary to all who would comprehend the problems, perils, challenges, and opportunities which confront us today." Thus, a study of history puts modern ideas and institutions in perspective. For example, though the founders of the United States were talented and creative thinkers, they clearly did not invent the concept of democracy. Instead, they adapted some democratic ideas that had originated in ancient Greece and with which the Romans, the British, and others had experimented. An exploration of these cultures, then, reveals their very real connection to us through institutions that continue to shape our daily lives.

Another reason often given for studying history is the idea that lessons exist in the past from which contemporary societies can benefit and learn. This idea, although controversial, has always been an intriguing one for historians. Those that agree that society can benefit from the past often quote philosopher George Santayana's famous statement, "Those who cannot remember the past are condemned to repeat it." Historians who ascribe to Santayana's philosophy believe that, for example, studying the events that led up to the major world wars or other significant historical events would allow society to chart a different and more favorable course in the future.

Just as difficult as convincing students to realize the importance of studying history is the search for useful and interesting supplementary materials that present historical events in a context that can be easily understood. The volumes in Lucent Books' World History Series attempt to present a broad, balanced, and penetrating view of the march of history. Ancient Egypt's important wars and rulers, for example, are presented against the rich and colorful backdrop of Egyptian religious, social, and cultural developments. The series engages the reader by enhancing historical events with these cultural contexts. For example, in *Ancient Greece*, the text covers the role of women in that society. Slavery is discussed in *The Roman Empire*, as well as how slaves earned their freedom. The numerous and varied aspects of everyday life in these and other societies are explored in each volume of the series. Additionally, the series covers the major political, cultural, and philosophical ideas as the torch of civilization is passed from ancient Mesopotamia and Egypt, through Greece, Rome, Medieval Europe, and other world cultures, to the modern day.

The material in the series is formatted in a thorough, precise, and organized manner. Each volume offers the reader a comprehensive and clearly written overview of an important historical event or period. The topic under discussion is placed in a broad historical context. For example, *The Italian Renaissance* begins with a discussion of the High Middle Ages and the loss of central control that allowed certain Italian cities to develop artistically. The book ends by looking forward to the Reformation and interpreting the societal changes that grew out of the Renaissance. Thus, students are not only involved in an historical era, but also enveloped by the events leading up to that era and the events following it.

One important and unique feature in the World History Series is the primary and secondary source quotations that richly supplement each volume. These quotes are useful in a number of ways. First, they allow students access to sources they would not normally be exposed to because of the difficulty and obscurity of the original source. The quotations range from interesting anecdotes to farsighted cultural perspectives and are drawn from historical witnesses both past and present. Second, the quotes demonstrate how and where historians themselves derive their information on the past as they strive to reach a consensus on historical events. Lastly, all of the quotes are footnoted, familiarizing students with the citation process and allowing them to verify quotes and/or look up the original source if the quote piques their interest.

Finally, the books in the World History Series provide a detailed launching point for further research. Each book contains a bibliography specifically geared toward student research. A second, annotated bibliography introduces students to all the sources the author consulted when compiling the book. A chronology of important dates gives students an overview, at a glance, of the topic covered. Where applicable, a glossary of terms is included.

In short, the series is designed not only to acquaint readers with the basics of history, but also to make them aware that their lives are a part of an ongoing human saga. Perhaps they will then come to the same realization as famed historian Arnold Toynbee. In his monumental work, *A Study of History,* he wrote about becoming aware of history flowing through him in a mighty current, and of his own life "welling like a wave in the flow of this vast tide."

Important Dates in the History of the Wars of the Roses

1376	1380	1385	1390	1395	1400	1405	1410	1415	1420	142

1376
Edward the Black Prince, oldest son of King Edward III of England, dies.

1377
King Edward III dies; Richard II, son of the Black Prince, becomes king of England.

1381
Peasants' Revolt in England.

1387
Five Lords Appellant take power from Richard II.

1389
Richard II declares himself able to rule on his own, dismisses Lords Appellant.

1397
Three of five Lords Appellant arrested.

1398
Remaining two Lords Appellant, including Henry of Bolingbroke, banished.

1399
John of Gaunt, duke of Lancaster and father of Henry of Bolingbroke, dies; Bolingbroke returns to England, deposes Richard II, and begins reign as King Henry IV.

1400
Richard II dies.

1413
Henry IV dies; Henry V becomes king of England.

1420
Treaty of Troyes makes Henry V heir to the throne of France; Henry V and Princess Catherine of France are married.

1422
Henry V dies; his infant son becomes King Henry VI of England.

1435
Henry VI's uncle, duke of Bedford, dies.

1445
Henry VI and Margaret of Anjou marry.

1447
Henry VI's uncle, duke of Gloucester, dies; Richard, duke of York, removed from command in France and appointed lieutenant of Ireland.

1450
Most English possessions in France lost; duke of Suffolk murdered; Cade's Rebellion breaks out in England; York returns from Ireland and takes power.

1451
Queen Margaret regains power.

1452
York's second attempt to gain power fails.

1453
Battle of Castillon in France ends Hundred Years' War; Henry VI suffers complete mental breakdown; son, Edward, born to Queen Margaret.

1454
York named protector to rule during Henry VI's illness; York loses power when Henry VI recovers.

1455
Wars of the Roses begin with First Battle of Saint Albans; duke of Somerset killed; Henry VI taken prisoner; Henry ill again and York named protector.

1456
Henry VI recovers; York dismissed as protector.

1458
Henry VI stages reconciliation ceremony between Yorks and Lancasters in London.

1459

Battle of Blore Heath won by Yorkists; York forced to flee to Ireland, and Warwick and York's son, Edward, to Calais.

1460

Warwick and March return to England and defeat Lancastrians at Battle of Northampton; Henry VI taken prisoner; York returns from Ireland and claims throne but is refused by Parliament; York killed as Lancastrians win Battle of Wakefield.

1461

Earl of March defeats Lancastrians at Battle of Mortimer's Cross; Queen Margaret's army defeats Yorkists at Second Battle of Saint Albans; earl of March claims throne and is accepted as Edward IV; Edward IV defeats Lancastrians at Battle of Towton.

1462

Margaret invades England from Scotland with a small force but flees to France when Edward IV approaches.

1463

Yorkist army wins Battle of Hedgeley Moor.

1464

Edward IV secretly marries Elizabeth Woodville; Yorkists win Battle of Hexham; duke of Somerset executed.

1465

Henry VI captured and imprisoned in Tower of London.

1469

Marriage of Edward IV's brother, duke of Clarence, and earl of Warwick's daughter, Isobel; Warwick and Clarence lead rebellion against Edward IV; Yorkists lose Battle of Edgecote; Edward IV taken prisoner but set free after a few months.

1470

Pro-Warwick rebels defeated by Edward IV at Battle of Losecoat Field; Warwick and Clarence flee to France; Warwick and Queen Margaret form alliance; Warwick and Clarence invade England with help of French king Louis XI; Edward IV flees to Burgundy; Henry VI restored to throne of England.

1471

Edward IV returns to England; Edward IV wins Battle of Barnet; Warwick killed; Edward wins Battle of Tewkesbury; Prince Edward killed; Henry VI killed in Tower of London.

1475

Treaty of Picquigny between Edward IV and Louis XI brings peace between England and France.

1479

Duke of Clarence executed in Tower of London.

1483

Edward IV dies; Gloucester and Buckingham take control of Edward V at Stony Stratford; Lord Hastings murdered; Gloucester crowned Richard III; Edward V and Prince Richard murdered in Tower of London; duke of Buckingham executed.

1484

Edward, Prince of Wales, only son of Richard III, dies.

1485

Queen Anne dies; Henry Tudor lands at Milford Haven; Richard III killed at Battle of Bosworth; Henry Tudor becomes King Henry VII.

A Family Affair

If wars are measured by death and destruction, the Wars of the Roses, fought in England during the thirty years from 1455 to 1485, did not amount to much. They were not really wars at all. They did not pit country against country. They were not wars of liberation in which people sought to gain their freedom. They were not fought for the sake of glory or for great wealth. Most of the people who took part wound up much poorer for their efforts.

What, then, were the Wars of the Roses? Basically, they were nothing more than a family feud, but that family happened to be the Plantagenets, rulers of England for three hundred years. At stake, as S. B. Chimes wrote, was "the greatest earthly prize within the reach of any of them—the crown of England with all the wealth, power, and influence that went with it."[1] And, as the Lancaster and York branches of the Plantagenets drifted into war, they brought with them most of the noble families of the country.

The conflict's name comes from the scene in William Shakespeare's play *Henry VI*, in which the two sides choose roses as their symbols—the red rose for the house of Lancaster and the white rose for the house of York. Even this is misleading. The white rose was one sign of Lancaster, but the red rose was not used until the house of Tudor came to the throne at the end of the war. The name Wars of the Roses was not used until 1762 in a history by David Hume.

In this age when war was supposed to be valorous, there was little noble about the Wars of the Roses. Brothers fought

A painting portraying the scene from William Shakespeare's play Henry VI *when the houses of Lancaster and York choose their rose symbols. The name Wars of the Roses was derived from this famous scene.*

brothers, fathers fought sons. Important prisoners were executed without trials. Battles were won, not by brilliant strategy or stirring feats of arms, but by last-minute deceit. As historian Charles Ross wrote, "The Wars of the Roses provide plenty of examples of rampant self-interest, of treachery and of cynical changes of side."[2]

Business as Usual

Although Edward Hall, a historian writing in 1548, bemoaned "what misery, what murder and what execrable [wretched] plagues" resulted from the conflict, little physical damage was actually done.[3] Unlike France, large areas of which had recently been laid waste during the Hundred Years' War, England suffered very little during the Wars of the Roses. No towns were burned; few castles were destroyed. The common people were hardly affected at all. Trade and commerce went on mostly as if nothing were happening.

Even the fighting itself was nowhere near as bloody as the writing of Edward Hall and the plays of William Shakespeare would indicate. One modern writer called the First Battle of Saint Albans "little more than a short scuffle in a street."[4] Many of the other battles involved only a few noblemen and their personal armies. Only Towton, where both sides together numbered about fifty thousand, could match the major battles of previous wars.

Consequently, relatively few soldiers were killed throughout the Wars of the Roses. Only about thirty thousand men died in the dozen or so battles spread over thirty years. During the Hundred Years'

Unlike the death and destruction caused in France by the Hundred Years' War (pictured), the Wars of the Roses had little effect on the common people of England.

War fifteen thousand men were killed at the Battle of Crécy alone. However, a high percentage of the lives lost—compared to other wars—were among the noble families of England. This was not a war of one class against another, but of one class against itself. The nobility of the country was heavily involved. Princes, dukes, and earls were killed in large numbers. Three kings met violent deaths.

The Wars of the Roses are important, therefore, because they altered the political, not the physical, landscape. The wars severely limited the power of the great nobles and, at the same time, increased the power of the king. They marked the end of the Middle Ages and the beginning of the Tudor period, the start of England's rise to world prominence.

1 The House of Lancaster

The king was not merely the center of government in medieval Europe; the king *was* the government. As historian A. L. Rowse wrote, "Everything depended upon the person of the monarch."[5] A strong king often meant victory in war abroad and peace and prosperity at home. A weak king meant rebellion, civil war, and internal turmoil as those around the throne fought for power. The house of Lancaster arose from just such circumstances.

The Plantagenet family, of which the Lancasters and Yorks were branches, first came to the throne when King Henry I of England died without a male heir in 1135. When Henry died, war broke out between his daughter, Matilda, and a nephew, Stephen of Blois. After twenty years of warfare it was decided that Stephen would rule but would be succeeded by Henry, son of Matilda and Geoffrey of Anjou, whose family name was Plantagenet, after a flower he wore in his hat.

The Plantagenets produced some of the strongest kings in English history, and Edward III was one of the most successful. His mother, Isabella, had been the last surviving child of King Philip IV of France. As a result, in 1339 the ambitious young English monarch claimed the throne of France. He sought to enforce his claim by starting what became the Hundred Years' War between the two countries.

Edward III was a brilliant general. In 1346 he invaded France and won an astounding victory at Crécy against overwhelming odds. His son, Edward the Black Prince—so called because of the color of

King Edward III was hailed as one of England's most successful monarchs. When he claimed the French throne in 1339, he started the Hundred Years' War between England and France.

A valiant soldier, Edward the Black Prince won many victories during the Hundred Years' War.

his armor—proved to be an even greater warrior. In 1356, at the age of twenty-six, he defeated a much larger French army at Poitiers and captured the French king, John II.

The Black Prince might have been as strong a king as his father, but he never had the chance. He caught a disease, probably dysentery, during a military campaign in Spain and was forced to return from France to England in 1372. He died in 1376 at the age of forty-three.

A Boy King

Edward III died the next year. Although he had three other sons still living, the rule of succession was that the crown should go to the Black Prince's son, Richard of Bordeaux. Richard was only ten years old, and the struggles for power that were to surround the boy king paved the way to revolution and, later, to the Wars of the Roses.

Richard was crowned King Richard II on July 16, 1377. As he rode through the streets of London in a glittering parade, he was accompanied by his three uncles—John of Gaunt, the duke of Lancaster; Edmund of Langley, later the duke of York; and Thomas of Woodstock, later the duke of Gloucester. Also in the procession was John of Gaunt's nine-year-old son, Henry of Bolingbroke, who would ultimately remove Richard from the throne.

The most powerful of these figures by far was John of Gaunt. In 1362 he had married Blanche, heiress of the fabulously wealthy earl of Lancaster, who had no sons. John was already rich, but his marriage made him—as duke of Lancaster—the

John of Gaunt, already the richest man in England, became regent for young King Richard II in 1377.

Thomas, duke of Gloucester, is visited by his nephew, King Richard II. Hoping to limit Richard's power, Gloucester plotted to kill the young king and make himself monarch of England.

richest man in England, richer even than the king. Now he ruled the country in his nephew's name.

At first it seemed as if Richard would develop into a strong, wise king. But he grew up to be vain, conceited, and extravagant. John of Gaunt was able to control his nephew during the first few years of his reign, but after 1384 John spent most of his time in France. With John gone, Richard began to spend money lavishly, even though the people were paying high taxes to finance the war in France. He favored peace with France, while most of the nobles wanted to continue the war. He showered titles, gifts, and promotions on a few favorites. He considered that, as king, his word was law, and he would not listen to advice.

Another royal uncle, Thomas, duke of Gloucester, was determined to limit Richard's power. In 1387, together with four other nobles—the earl of Arundel, the earl of Warwick, Thomas Mowbray, and Henry of Bolingbroke—Gloucester demanded that Richard dismiss his favorites and put himself under their control. Richard was forced to agree. Gloucester actually had wanted to kill Richard and make himself king. Arundel and Warwick agreed, but Mowbray and Bolingbroke refused to go that far. The five men came to be known as the Lords Appellant, because they later appealed to Parliament, England's legislative assembly, to approve their actions.

Richard's Surprise

Two years later, however, Richard sprang a surprise. One day during a meeting of his council, he calmly asked how old he was. Finally, Gloucester answered, "Three and twenty years." "Then," said Richard, "I am old enough to manage my own affairs."[6] He calmly demanded that Arundel turn over to him the Great Seal of England, used to give all official documents the force of law. Arundel had no choice but to comply. Not to do so would have been open treason.

At first Richard did not seek revenge against the five men who had humiliated him. It was not until 1397 that he felt strong enough to strike. Gloucester, Arundel, and Warwick were arrested. Arundel was beheaded, and Warwick was banished. Not wishing to place a royal duke on trial, Richard sent Gloucester to prison. Soon thereafter it was announced that Gloucester had died, probably smothered to death at Richard's command. Henry and Mowbray were later banished from England.

Richard had become a tyrant. He surrounded himself with a body of archers from the county of Chester, who were

> very evil; and in all places they oppressed his subjects unpunished, and

beat and robbed them . . . everywhere committing adulteries, murders and other evils without end. And to such a pass [an extent] did the King cherish them that he would not deign [condescend] to listen to anyone who had complaint against them.[7]

He forced his nobles to give him huge sums of money in the form of loans he never intended to repay. He made up lists of possible enemies and made them put their seals on blank charters. He could then ensure their good behavior by threatening to fill in these charters as

The Tyranny of Richard II

One reason that Henry of Bolingbroke was able to overthrow King Richard II was the unrest caused by Richard's harsh rule. Richard's method of obtaining money is described in this passage from Thomas Walsingham's fifteenth-century history of England, found in English Historical Documents, *edited by A. R. Myers.*

"In the same year [1399] he demanded greater sums of money from seventeen shires [counties] of the realm, under fear of death, charging them that they had supported the Duke of Gloucester, and the Earls of Arundel and Warwick in their opposition to him; wherefore he was ready to ride against them, as if they were public enemies. On this account he received from the shires new security under oath. When this had been done, he sent certain bishops, with other honourable men, to the shires, to induce the lords spiritual [the higher clergy] and temporal [the nobles], and all the middling ranks of the shires, to submit to the king and acknowledge themselves as traitors by letters sealed with their seals. For this reason the clergy and commonality, and all the temporal lords of the shires were compelled to pay to the king insupportable sums of money, to recover his favour. The king desiring, as it was said, to subdue and oppress the people of his realm, directed letters patent [royal orders] to all shires of his realm, and induced them by terror, both temporal and clerical subjects, to swear unconditional oaths of a kind which could really cause the final destruction of his people, and forced his lieges [those under him] to confirm these oaths under their letters and seals. He compelled them to affix their seals to blank charters [sheets of paper], so that, as often as he might wish to proceed against them, he should have the opportunity to oppress them singly or together."

confessions of crimes against the throne. A French writer of the time, Jean de Froissart, wrote, "At this time, there was nobody in England, however great, that dared speak out about the actions or intentions of the king."[8]

Finally Richard went too far. In February 1399 John of Gaunt died. Richard took advantage of Henry of Bolingbroke's absence to seize all the lands that were Henry's rightful inheritance. Now even many of the nobles loyal to Richard turned against him. If the king could seize the vast holdings of Lancaster, no man's property was safe.

The Return of York

Richard's second great mistake was to leave the country at a time of such discord, embarking on a military expedition to Ireland. He left England in the care of his meek, incompetent uncle, Edmund, duke of York. Henry, now duke of Lancaster, seized the opportunity. With a small company of knights, he sailed from France and on July 4 landed in the town of Ravenspur on the Yorkshire coast in the far north of England. He had come not to overthrow the king, he said, but only to regain what was rightfully his—the duchy of Lancaster. As more and more nobles came to join him, however, he realized the throne could be his.

When Richard learned of Henry's landing in England, he hurried back from Ireland with his troops. Most of his soldiers deserted, however, when they learned the extent of Henry's support. Richard was at the mercy of his cousin. They met at Flint Castle in north Wales.

"Your people, my lord," said Henry, "complain that you have ruled them harshly. However, if it please God, I will help you rule them better."

"Fair cousin," answered Richard after a long silence, "since it pleases you, it pleases me well."[9]

On September 30 Richard was taken to Westminster Hall in London. There he read a paper announcing that he was surrendering the throne. Then a long list of accusations against him was read. Finally, he handed the crown and the scepter of office to Henry and left the hall. Henry then rose and said:

> In the name of Father, Son and Holy Ghost, I, Henry of Lancaster, challenge the realm of England, and the crown, with all the members and appurtenances [the many royal offices and de-

Following the death of his father, John of Gaunt, Henry of Bolingbroke returned from banishment to claim the Lancaster duchy.

(Right) After receiving the crown and scepter of office from deposed king Richard II, Henry, duke of Lancaster (below), accepts the throne as King Henry IV.

partments]; as that I am descended by the right line of blood, coming from the good lord Henry III [Edward III's great-grandfather], and through that right that God of His grace has sent me with the help of my kin and of my friends to recover it; the which realm [England] was in point to be [on the brink of] undone for default of governance and undoing of good laws.[10]

He was then led to the throne and proclaimed King Henry IV.

Henry's Problems

There were two problems. First, Henry was not the rightful heir to the throne. The young Edmund de Mortimer, earl of March, was the grandson of Philippa, daughter of Edward III's second son, Lionel. His heritage gave him precedence over Henry, a descendant of John of Gaunt, Edward's third son. This fact was simply ignored at the time but later would become important in the Wars of the Roses. It did, however, cast a shadow over Henry IV's reign, since everyone knew he had taken the throne illegally.

The other problem was that the former king, Richard, was still alive and might become the center of a revolt in the future. This problem was not ignored. Richard was sent as a prisoner to Pontefract Castle in the north. In February 1400 it was announced that he had died, probably murdered on Henry's orders. Richard's death, and that of his uncle, the duke of Gloucester, set the pattern for a series of royal murders that would characterize the Wars of the Roses.

During his short but successful reign, King Henry V (below) displayed his military prowess by invading France and renewing the English claim to the French throne (left).

The reign of Henry IV was unhappy. Parliament, which had upheld Henry's questionable right to the throne, demanded changes in the government. Henry faced several rebellions, including one in Wales led by Owen Glendower. His health failed. More and more the country was governed by his son, Prince Henry, and the king's half-brothers—John, Henry, and Thomas Beaufort.

The Beauforts were illegitimate sons of John of Gaunt and his mistress, Catherine Swynford. John eventually married Catherine and convinced King Richard to declare their children legitimate. The Beauforts were to become one of the most powerful families in England and would play major roles in the Wars of the Roses.

Henry IV died in 1413. Many people at the time said his life was shortened by his guilt over Richard's murder. His son, Henry V, became one of the strongest and most successful kings in the history of England. The Wars of the Roses, however, came about as a direct result of his conquest of France, his marriage, and his premature death.

Henry V renewed the claim of Edward III to the French throne. He invaded France in 1415 and won a tremendous victory at Agincourt. He launched another successful invasion in 1417, ending in the Treaty of Troyes in 1420. Under this treaty Henry would marry Catherine, daughter of King Charles VI of France, and would succeed Charles on the French throne.

Another Boy King

Henry and Catherine were married in June 1420. A little more than two years later, Henry was dead. He left behind a son, also named Henry, who had been born at Windsor Castle in December 1421. This child, Henry VI, ascended the thrones of both England and France. For the second time in fifty years, England had a boy king. That was bad enough. What nobody yet knew was that the new king—now less than a year old—had inherited the frail health and weak mind of his French grandfather, Charles VI. Though Henry VI would reign for many years, he would never be a strong ruler. He would grow up to be mild mannered, overly merciful to enemies, indecisive, easily led by others—everything a strong king in the Middle Ages should not be. Historian Charles Ross wrote that if Henry VI "had been half the man his father was, the disasters that followed . . . might easily have been avoided."[11]

The Gentle King

In an age when successful kings were mighty warriors, shrewd politicians, and lavish spenders, Henry VI of England was the exact opposite. This description of him, written by his chaplain, a monk named John Blacman, is found in The Wars of the Roses, *by J. R. Lander.*

"He was . . . a man simple and upright, altogether fearing the Lord God, and departing from evil. He was a simple man, without any crook [inclination] of craft or untruth, as is plain to all. With none did he deal craftily, nor ever would say an untrue word to any, but framed his speech always to speak truth. . . . A diligent and sincere worshipper of God was this king, more given to God and to devout prayer than to handling worldly and temporal things, or practising vain sports and pursuits: these he despised as trifling, and was continually occupied either in prayer or the reading of the scriptures or of chronicles [histories], whence he drew not a few wise utterances to the spiritual comfort of himself and others. . . . Further of his humility in his bearing, in his clothes and other apparel of his body, in his speech and many other parts of his outward behaviour—it is well known that from his youth up he always wore round-toed shoes and boots like a farmer's. He also customarily wore a long gown with a rolled hood like a townsman, and a full coat reaching below his knees, with shoes, boots and foot-gear wholly black, rejecting expressly all curious fashion of clothing."

For most of Henry VI's childhood, things went smoothly, thanks mostly to the abilities of his uncle John, duke of Bedford, who shared the title Lord Protector and Defender of the Realm along with another royal uncle, Humphrey, duke of Gloucester. With the death of Bedford in 1435, however, a struggle for power in England broke out between those who wanted peace with France and those who wanted to continue the war. Heading the peace party were Henry Beaufort, bishop of Winchester; his nephew Edmund Beaufort, duke of Somerset; and Michael de la Pole, the duke of Suffolk. The war party was led by Gloucester, the young king's uncle.

The Beauforts were successful in getting Parliament to reduce the amount of money spent on the war. This action earned them a new enemy, Richard, duke of York, who was the military commander in France. York, one of the central figures

As Lord Protector and Defender of the Realm, John, duke of Bedford (pictured), ably ruled England for his nephew, King Henry VI.

in the Wars of the Roses, was the grandson of Edmund of Langley, son of Edward III. He was also, however, the great-grandson of Edward's second son, Lionel. Technically, therefore, York had a better claim to the throne than Henry VI, who was descended from Edward's third son, John of Gaunt.

The Beauforts forced York to pay much of the cost of the war out of his own purse. In 1441 Henry VI signed a decree ordering "great and notable sums of money" to repay York what he had spent on his troops, but it proved to be an empty promise.[12] York was further angered the next year when Somerset was sent to France as York's superior.

Seeking a Queen

The peace party had one major worry. Henry VI, now in his early twenties, was unmarried, and the heir to the throne was the Beauforts' enemy, Gloucester. The Beauforts needed Henry to have a wife who would bear him a son. Also, knowing that the meek king would be dominated by whomever he married, they wanted a wife who would be their political ally. And finally, wanting peace with France, they sought a French bride for Henry.

In 1444 Suffolk was sent to France to find a wife for his king. His choice was Margaret, daughter of the noble but poor Duke René of Anjou, whose sister was queen of France. The king of France knew how important the marriage was to Suffolk and as a condition got him to promise that the English would withdraw from the French county of Maine.

Margaret was already famous for her beauty. What Suffolk could not yet see was

Soon after the marriage of Henry VI and Margaret of Anjou in 1445, the young queen took control of her husband's affairs, dominating the English monarchy.

her strong personality. She would become, in writer Franklin Hamilton's words, "so fiery, so determined, so savage in the defense of her lawful rights that she brought the dynasty of Lancaster to ruin and presided over the wreckage of a divided England."[13]

Margaret and Henry were married in 1445, and the fourteen-year-old queen quickly gained complete control over her twenty-three-year-old husband. She was thoroughly French in her sympathies and wanted to end the war. She regarded the Beauforts and Suffolk as her friends, York and Gloucester as her enemies.

In February 1447 Gloucester learned of the agreement to turn Maine over to the French. He began to speak out bitterly against the plan. By that time, however, Margaret and her friends had succeeded in limiting Gloucester's power. The duke was arrested. Five days later came the announcement that he was dead. People whispered that Margaret had ordered him murdered.

Bishop Beaufort died that same year, leaving Somerset and Suffolk the leaders of what was now the queen's party. Only one man, Richard of York, remained who was powerful enough to challenge their authority. In September 1447 they removed York from his command in France and gave him a ten-year appointment as lieutenant of Ireland, hoping to get him out of the way. York went to Ireland with his wife, Cicely Neville, and their five children, including seven-year-old Edward, earl of March, and six-year-old Edmund, earl of Rutland.

The Death of Suffolk

In England things went from bad to worse. In 1448 Maine was formally handed over to the French, infuriating most English. In

1449 the French king, Charles VII, resumed the war, and by August 1450 England, whose army was led by Somerset, had lost all possessions in France except the city of Calais and the province of Guienne. An angry Parliament wanted Suffolk executed, but Queen Margaret got Henry to change the sentence to banishment, hoping to restore him later. As Suffolk sailed from England, however, he was intercepted by a ship from the royal navy. Suffolk's head was forced down on a wooden block and hacked off with six strokes from a rusty sword. There was some evidence that York had planned the murder.

York also was thought to have been behind the wave of violence that soon swept England. Its leader, a man named Jack Cade, spoke out in the southern county of Kent against the losses in France, high taxes, and the lavish gifts given to Margaret's favorites. He marched on London, gathering more rebels as he went. After Cade's group defeated a royal army, the king, queen, and most of the court fled from London, which Cade cap-

The Death of Suffolk

When Parliament, angry over the loss of the province of Maine in France, wanted Queen Margaret's favorite, the duke of Suffolk, who had negotiated the treaty with the French, executed, she convinced King Henry VI to change the punishment to banishment. Suffolk sailed for France but never arrived, as this excerpt from a letter written by William Lomner shows. It is found in The Wars of the Roses, *by J. R. Lander.*

"The master of the Nicholas [*Nicholas of the Tower*, a ship] had knowledge of [Suffolk's] coming. And when he espied the duke's ships, he sent forth his boat to weet [see] what they were, and the duke himself spake to them, and said he was by the king's commandment sent to Calais. And they said he must speak with their master. And so he, with two or three of his men, went forth with them in their boat to the Nicholas; and when he come, the master bade him, 'Welcome, Traitor,' as men say. . . . Some say he was arraigned [put on trial] in the ship on here manner upon the appeachments [charges of treason] and found guilty. . . . And in the sight of all his men he was drawn out of the great ship into the boat; and there was an axe, and a stroke, and one of the lewdest [most lowly sailors] of the ship bade him lay down his head, and he should be fair ferd with [treated fairly], and die on a sword; and took a rusty sword, and smote off his head within half a dozen strokes, and took away his gown of russet [red], and his doublet [jacket] of velvet mayled [covered with metal rings], and laid his body on the sands of Dover; and some say his head was set on a pole by it, and his men set on the land by great circumstance and praye."

A captured noble is brought before rebellion leader Jack Cade (seated). Cade and his rebels initiated a violent protest against the rule of King Henry and Queen Margaret.

tured on July 1, 1450. Following a weekend of terror the citizens of London organized and attacked the rebels. An eyewitness wrote to a friend, "There was fighting upon London Bridge, and many a man was slain or cast in Thames, harness [armor], body and all."[14] Finally Cade and his men agreed to lay down their arms and return home in exchange for pardons. The pardons were soon revoked, and Cade was hunted down and killed as a traitor.

Jack Cade was dead, but the rebellion had spread to other parts of the kingdom. The people wanted a strong leader to re-store order. More and more their thoughts turned to Richard of York. York was still in Ireland, but there was a clause in his orders that permitted him to return to England in case of a national emergency. Clearly, this latest turmoil was such a case, and it gave him an opportunity to get revenge on the Beauforts.

In August 1450 York sailed across the Irish Sea with a small force and landed in Wales. Margaret, alarmed by the reappearance of her enemy, recalled Somerset from France. For the first time the forces of Lancaster and York faced one another, setting the stage for the Wars of the Roses.

2 The Duke and the Queen

For the five years from 1450 to 1455, King Henry VI of England was at the center of a tug-of-war for power between his wife, Queen Margaret, and his cousin, Richard of York. Although there was no actual fighting, the division of the country into two factions—Lancaster and York—quickened. The two sides were clearly headed for war.

Margaret could be blamed for much of this. She was as strong in her hatreds as in her loyalties. Had she allowed her husband to be an impartial ruler, deciding between rival factions, the Wars of the Roses might have never occurred. But Margaret could not help taking sides. As one biographer wrote:

> She never learned to play the part of a mediator, or to raise the Crown above the fierce factional [partisan] fight that constantly raged around Henry's Court. In identifying her husband completely with the one faction, she almost forced the rival party into opposition to the King and to the dynasty.[15]

When York returned from Ireland in 1450, no one knew if he had come to claim the throne or to help put an end to the disorders created by Cade's Rebellion. Margaret took no chances. She sent agents to intercept York and assassinate him. He was warned of her plan, evaded the force sent against him, and reached his castle at Ludlow, near the English-Welsh border. He remained there several months, evaluating the situation and gathering troops from those nobles opposed to Margaret and Somerset.

During the reign of King Henry VI, England was torn between the Lancastrian faction of Queen Margaret (pictured) and the Yorkist faction of Richard.

Parliament was due to meet in London in November. With an army at his back, York went to London and demanded to see King Henry. He pledged his loyalty, saying he had returned only to put an end to Somerset's evil influence. He asked Henry why he had allowed the queen to send men to murder him. Henry evaded the question, saying only, "We declare you our true subject and faithful cousin."[16]

Parliament welcomed York as a person who could bring peace. It ordered Somerset's arrest and called for York to be the head of the royal council. Margaret persuaded Henry to send Somerset to the Tower of London, not as a prisoner, but to keep him safe from York's followers. York, thinking he had accomplished his mission, returned to Ludlow as Parliament ended. With York out of the way, Margaret quickly had Somerset released and named him to the important military posts of constable of England and captain of Calais. Parliament's demands were ignored.

When Parliament met the next year, a lawyer named Thomas Young, a follower of York, declared that since Henry and Margaret were childless after six years of marriage, York should be named heir to the throne. It was now evident to the Lancasters that York wanted nothing less than to be king. At Margaret's urging Henry ordered Parliament dissolved and Young thrown into prison.

Somerset Accused

In 1452 York publicly announced his intention to force Somerset from office. He accused Somerset of "laboring continually about the King's Highness for my undo-ing, and to corrupt my blood, and to disinherit me and my heirs." He ended by writing:

> I signify unto you that with the help and supportation [support] of Almighty God . . . I, after long sufferance [patience] and delays, not my will or intent to displease my sovereign lord, seeing that the said duke [Somerset] ever prevaileth and ruleth about the king's person, that by this means the land is likely to be destroyed, am fully concluded to proceed in all haste against him, with the help of my kinsmen and friends.[17]

York assembled an army and marched toward London. Margaret and Somerset raised an even larger force and convinced the mild King Henry to put on armor and lead it in person. When York found that Henry was leading the opposition, he halted a short distance from the city. He did not dare attack the king. When Henry sent a message asking that he come for a discussion, York went to the king's camp, accompanied by forty knights. York insisted that Somerset be brought to trial, as had been ordered by Parliament in 1450. Henry said it would be done if York disbanded his army.

York believed his king. He told his knights to ride back to his army and tell the soldiers to go home. No sooner had this been done than York was taken prisoner. Margaret and Somerset would have liked to execute him but did not dare. York was too popular with the people. Instead they forced him to appear in Saint Paul's Cathedral in London and to swear allegiance to Henry and to raise no more troops. Outwitted and humiliated, York returned to Ludlow.

Strained by growing discontent over England's defeat in the Hundred Years' War, Henry VI suffered a complete mental breakdown in 1453.

Three events occurred in 1453 that dramatically changed the situation. First, the Hundred Years' War ended. On July 17 the English army was destroyed by the French at the town of Castillon in Guienne. Within months England, which once had controlled half of France, had only the city of Calais to show for 118 years of warfare.

England was stunned. The people were angry. To calm them, Henry and Margaret went on visits throughout the country to reassure the people and to gain support. The strain was more than Henry's feeble mind could take, bringing on the second great event of 1453. The king suffered a complete mental breakdown. Day after day he sat looking at the ground—saying nothing, recognizing no one, understanding nothing. His state was much like that experienced by his grandfather, King Charles VI of France.

An Heir to the Crown

In October the third event occurred. Margaret gave birth to a son, Prince Edward. Even this event could not rouse Henry from his stupor. Indeed, many people said Henry was not the child's father. They whispered that Margaret, desperate for a child to be Henry's heir, had become Somerset's lover.

When Henry failed to recover his senses, Parliament met early in 1454 to name a protector to rule England. Margaret asked that the power be given to her, but most of the nobles did not trust her or Somerset. They gave the title, instead, to Richard of York. York, they reasoned, now would have no claim on the throne since Prince Edward was Henry's lawful heir. York acted swiftly. Somerset was arrested and imprisoned in the Tower of London. Officials who had been appointed by the Beauforts were dismissed and their places taken by Yorkists. York himself took the post of captain of Calais, which was important because the port city in France could be a point from which to launch an invasion of England.

The frustrated Margaret, now completely devoted to protecting the life and rights of her son, began to gather allies, all of them nobles opposed to York. She could take no action, however, as long as York held power. Her opportunity came around Christmas of 1454 when Henry suddenly regained his senses.

With the king sane once more, York had no excuse to continue in power. He resigned as protector and returned to Ludlow. Margaret and Somerset had regained power and were determined to use it. They called on the country's leading nobles to meet in council "for the purpose of providing the safety of the king's person against his enemies."[18]

Chief among the king's enemies, in Margaret's view, were York and his two main allies—Richard Neville, earl of Salisbury, and his son Richard, earl of Warwick—father and brother of York's wife, Cicely. The Nevilles, a large and powerful family from the north of England, had been closely allied with the Beauforts. When the Beauforts showed more favor to the Nevilles' great rivals, the Percy family, the Nevilles allied themselves with York.

This pattern of families embroiled in private quarrels gradually moving either to the Lancastrian or Yorkist side repeated itself throughout the country.

The War Begins

York, Salisbury, and Warwick had not been invited to the council. Fearing that some action would be planned against them, they decided to act first. With an army of about five thousand men, they marched

---

The King Recovers

In 1453 King Henry VI suffered a mental breakdown that lasted more than a year and enabled the duke of York to gain control of the kingdom. Henry's recovery was described in a letter written by a man named Edmund Clere to an acquaintance. This excerpt is found in The Wars of the Roses, *by J. R. Lander.*

"Blessed be God, the King is well amended, and hath been since Christmas day, and on St. John's day commanded his almoner [a priest] to ride to Canterbury with his offering, and commanded the secretary to offer [make an offering] at St. Edward's. And on the Monday after noon the Queen came to him, and brought My Lord Prince [their son Edward] with her. And then he asked what the Prince's name was, and the Queen told him Edward; and then he held up his hands and thanked God thereof. And he said he never knew till that time, nor wist [understood] not what was said to him, nor wist not where he had [been] whilst he hath [been] sick till now. . . . And she told him that the Cardinal [John Kemp, archbishop of Canterbury] was dead, and he said he knew never thereof till that time; and he said one of the wisest lords in this land was dead. And my Lord of Winchester and my Lord of St. John's were with him on the morrow after Twelfth Day [January 6], and he speke to them as well as ever he did; and when they come out they wept for joy. And he saith he is in charity with all the world, and so he would [wish that] all the lords were."

---

on London. Somerset, taking King Henry with him, led a force about half that size to meet them. The two sides met at the town of Saint Albans about twenty-five miles north of London on May 22, 1455.

Somerset's troops reached the unwalled town first and set up barricades across the main streets. When York reached the town, he sent a message calling on Henry to "deliver up such as we accuse [Somerset]. . . . We will not now slack until we have them, or else we, therefore, to die." Somerset answered for Henry, calling York and his allies traitors and saying, "I shall destroy them, every mother's son."[19]

York would not be put off any longer, and thus the Wars of the Roses began.

York charged down one main street toward one barricade while Salisbury charged toward the other. The streets were so narrow that their soldiers were brought to a halt. Then Warwick, whose troops were held back in reserve, noticed that a ditch between the two streets was mostly undefended. He seized his opportunity and led his men in a charge across the ditch, shouting his battle cry "A Warwick! A Warwick!" and burst through some private gardens into the town.[20]

With Warwick's troops attacking Somerset from behind, York and Salisbury were able to break through. Hand-to-hand fighting raged up and down the streets of Saint Albans for three hours. King Henry,

Lancastrian and Yorkist soldiers crowd the narrow streets of Saint Albans as the Wars of the Roses begin.

sitting bewildered on a horse in the midst of the struggle, was grazed in the shoulder by an arrow. Somerset was cut down by a Yorkist ax outside a tavern. When the battle was over, the Yorkists had won a complete victory.

York went before Henry and, kneeling, pledged his loyalty and begged forgiveness "for whatever way he might have offended and for the peril in which he had put his [Henry's] person."[21] Dazed and confused, Henry pardoned York and meekly allowed himself to be taken to London, a virtual prisoner. Margaret, hearing of the defeat, took refuge in the royal palace at Greenwich, east of London, with her son.

For four years after the Saint Albans battle there was an uneasy truce. First, Henry fell ill again late in 1455, and York was made protector. The king recovered after about three months, and York was dismissed. He was too strong, however, for Margaret to risk trying to arrest him. Also, Warwick continued to hold command of Calais, to which York had appointed him while acting as protector. The two sides watched each other warily, each gathering as much strength as it could.

Henry's "Unity Day"

The gentle Henry tried to bring the hostility to an end. In 1458 he arranged a unity day, a public ceremony that was supposed to signal a time of peace. A magnificent procession was staged in London. Salisbury marched hand in hand with Henry Beaufort, the new duke of Somerset after his father's death. Warwick marched with the Lancastrian duke of Exeter, and, last,

Margaret and York walked together, smiling to the crowd. At Saint Paul's Cathedral, a poem was read:

> At Paul's in London with great renown
> On Our Lady Day in Lent this peace
> was wrought;
> The king, the queen, with lords many
> a one,
> To worship that Virgin as they ought
> Went a procession and spared right
> nought,
> In sight of all the commonality,
> In token that love was in heart and
> thought.
> Rejoice, England, in concord and
> unity.[22]

The ceremony was a hollow farce, and everyone knew it except the childlike king. Whatever concord, harmony, and unity there were did not last long. By the spring of 1459 both Margaret and York were gathering as many troops as they could. In August Salisbury and his army marched from the north to join York at Ludlow. Margaret sent an army to intercept them, but Salisbury won a decisive victory at Blore Heath on September 23 and was able to reach York. He was also joined by Warwick, who had crossed the English Channel from Calais with a large body of professional soldiers. Also prominent among the Yorkist leaders were the duke's two oldest sons, seventeen-year-old Edward of March—a handsome giant of six foot three—and sixteen-year-old Edmund of Rutland.

Margaret had assembled the main body of her army at the city of Coventry, and from there it marched on Ludlow, reaching York's castle on October 12. Royal heralds rode up to the gate, offering King Henry's pardon to all who would desert York. After dark most of Warwick's

The First Battle of Saint Albans

The Wars of the Roses, brewing for years, finally broke out when the armies of Richard, duke of York, and Edmund Beaufort, duke of Somerset, met in the little town of Saint Albans. The following account, written soon after the battle by a French visitor, was found in archives at Dijon, France. It is printed in J. R. Lander's The Wars of the Roses.

"The battle began on the stroke of ten hours in the morning but because the place was small few of the combatants could set to work there and matters reached such great extremity that four of those who were of the king's [Henry VI's] bodyguard were killed by arrows in his presence and the king himself was struck by an arrow in the shoulder, but it penetrated only a little of the flesh. At last when they had fought for the space of three hours the king's party seeing themselves to have the worst of it broke on one wing and began to flee and the duke of Somerset retreated within an inn to save himself and hid. Which things seen by those of the said duke of York [they immediately] beset the said house [the inn] all about. And there the duke of York gave order that the king should be taken and drawn out of the throng and put in the abbey in safety and thus it was done. And in this abbey took refuge also with him the duke of Buckingham who was very badly wounded by three arrows. And [immediately] this done [they] began to fight Somerset and his men who were in the place within the inn and defended themselves valiantly. And in the end after the doors were broken down the duke of Somerset seeing that he had no other remedy took counsel with his men about coming out and did so, as a result of which [immediately] he and all his people were surrounded by the duke of York's men. And after some were stricken down and the duke of Somerset had killed four of them with his own hand, so it is said, he was felled to the ground with an axe and . . . being so wounded in several places that there he ended his life."

men, led by a captain named Andrew Trollope, rushed from the castle and surrendered to Margaret's army.

Now York faced certain defeat. He had no choice except to flee. Leaving his wife and their two younger sons, George and Richard, York slipped from Ludlow. Along with Warwick, Salisbury, and his sons Edward and Edmund, he rode toward Wales. There they separated. York and Edmund headed west to the coast, hired a boat, and went to Ireland. Warwick, Salisbury, and Edward went south to Devon. They also hired a boat and, with Warwick steering since no member of the crew had enough experience, sailed to Calais.

The Parliament of Devils

Margaret was now firmly in control. In November she assembled a Parliament dominated by Lancastrians. Later the Yorkists would call it the Parliament of Devils. York, Salisbury, Warwick, and March were attainted; that is, they were sentenced to death, all their property seized, and their descendants prohibited from inheriting either titles or property. A pamphlet published at the time accused the Yorkists

> of a pure malice and longtime precogitate [preplanned] wickedness, the which after the first indulgence had relapse[d] and recay in a greater and more pernicious [wicked] offense than the first was . . . doing such deeds with such circumstances that no very true man can it ascribe to any other purpose but to the final destruction of this gracious king and to the irreparable subversion of all his true lovers [supporters].[23]

Margaret knew she could not rest as long as York and Warwick were at large. She ordered a fleet to sail to Calais to capture Warwick. It was to be commanded by Richard Woodville, Lord Rivers, who had once been on the staff of the duke of Bedford, John of Lancaster, and who had been granted a title after he shocked everyone by marrying Bedford's widow,

Jacquetta, in 1337. The Woodvilles would later become major figures in the Wars of the Roses.

Rivers's fleet never sailed. Warwick, informed of Margaret's plan, raided Rivers's ships as they sat at anchor in the English port of Sandwich. Rivers and his son, Anthony, were captured and taken to Calais, where they were mocked by Warwick, Salisbury, and Edward of March.

Warwick now felt secure enough to sail to Ireland and meet with York to plan Margaret's overthrow. He then returned to Calais and on June 26, 1460, crossed to Sandwich with Salisbury, March, and two thousand troops. There they were welcomed by "a great multitude of people."[24]

After driving York, Warwick, and Salisbury out of England, Queen Margaret was once again in control. She then plotted to capture Warwick and quell any attempt at overthrow.

They marched to London, and by the time they reached the capital, the army had swelled to six thousand. The Londoners, unhappy with the favoritism shown to foreign merchants by Henry's government, opened the city gates to the invaders, who then marched north to confront Henry and Margaret.

Margaret had not been idle. She had gathered troops loyal to the king at Coventry, north of London. This army marched south and met Warwick and March (Salisbury had remained in London) near the town of Northampton on July 10. The royal army was in a fortified position and had brought several cannons, which had only recently become a truly effective weapon of war. Warwick sent a messenger to Henry, demanding to see the king. The duke of Buckingham sent back the reply: "The Earl of Warwick shall not come into the King's presence, and if he comes he shall die."[25]

Warwick (pictured), along with two thousand troops, confronted Henry VI and Queen Margaret near the town of Northampton on July 10, 1460.

The Battle of Northampton

At two o'clock in the afternoon, Warwick's army charged. By half past two the Battle of Northampton was over because of a combination of weather and treachery. Heavy rains had made the royalists' cannons useless. Also, Warwick had been in secret contact with Lord Grey of Ruthyn, a Lancastrian noble who commanded the part of Henry's army that faced Edward of March's troops. At a signal, Grey's soldiers threw down their weapons and helped Edward's men climb over the barricade. The royalists were quickly forced back into the Nene River, in which more than three hundred drowned. Buckingham was killed, and poor King Henry was once more captured.

Richard of York had remained in Ireland all this time, waiting for the right moment to return. He chose October, when Parliament was to meet in London. He entered the city in a great procession, bearing not his own coat of arms, but those of the king of England. He announced that since he was descended from Edward III's

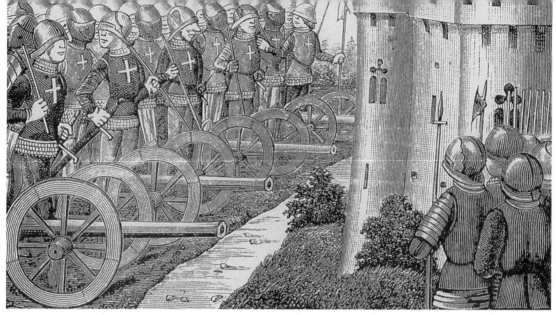

Cannons proved effective during the Hundred Years' War (pictured); however, heavy rains rendered this relatively new weapon useless during the Battle of Northampton.

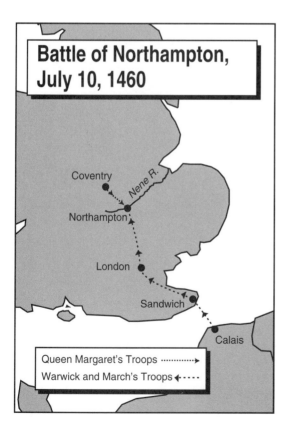

Battle of Northampton, July 10, 1460

Coventry

Nene R.

Northampton

London

Sandwich

Calais

Queen Margaret's Troops ··········➤
Warwick and March's Troops ◄····

second son, the throne was rightfully his and he had come to claim it.

York strode into Westminster Hall, where Parliament was meeting, placed his hand on the throne, and turned toward the assembly, expecting it to cheer him. Instead he faced only silence. The nobles had wanted him to rule England *for* Henry, not to take Henry's place. They hated Margaret but were loyal to their anointed king. Finally, the archbishop of Canterbury, England's highest church official, asked York if he had come to see the king. York responded: "I do not recall anyone I know within the kingdom whom it would not befit to come sooner to me and see me than I should go and visit him." [26]

York took the king's apartments for himself, having moved Henry to those formerly occupied by Margaret. He demanded that Parliament make him king, but it refused. Even Warwick and Salisbury were angry. They had intended only to overthrow Margaret. At last Parliament declared that Henry would remain king but that York would be named his heir.

This solution might have worked had it not been for the iron will of Queen Margaret. After the Battle of Northampton she and Prince Edward had fled north with a few servants. They were attacked by armed bandits. The servants ran, and the bandits began to loot Margaret's baggage. The queen thought she would be killed and decided on a desperate appeal to a young robber who looked less bloodthirsty than the rest. Putting the seven-year-old Edward in the man's arms, she pleaded, "Save the son of your king."[27] The robber sneaked her away from his colleagues and saw her safely to the Welsh castle of Jasper Tudor.

Tudor and his brother Edmund were half brothers of King Henry. The widow of Henry V, Catherine of France, had fallen in love with and married a poor soldier in her household named Owen Tudor. Their children included Jasper and Edmund. The Tudors would later play a major role in the Wars of the Roses.

Margaret Fights Back

Margaret was not one to stand by and see her son disinherited. She began to gather the nobles loyal to the house of Lancaster—the Tudors, the young duke of Somerset, the Percy family, the Cliffords— and within months had a large army of about twenty thousand. With Margaret taking personal command, this army began to attack some of the Neville lands in the northern county of Yorkshire.

York decided to meet this threat head-on but had little idea of Margaret's strength. He and his son Edmund of Rutland headed north at the head of a force of about only six thousand. When he came in contact with the queen's army and found himself outnumbered, he retreated to Sandal Castle, one of his fortresses in Yorkshire. Sandal was heavily fortified, and York could have safely stayed there while waiting for March and Warwick to bring reinforcements. Instead, on December 30 he rashly went out to meet his enemies in what would come to be known as the Battle of Wakefield, a nearby town.

Margaret had positioned the Lancastrian troops herself. She had ordered the center of her forces to fall back on pur-

Fearing she would be killed by bandits, Queen Margaret desperately pleaded with a young robber to save her son, seven-year-old Prince Edward.

Following her victory over the Yorkists, Queen Margaret had York, Salisbury, and Rutland beheaded. This fanciful painting shows Margaret mocking York by placing a paper crown on his head.

pose before York's charge. Then her mounted cavalry, which had been concealed behind a hill, charged from the side. The badly outnumbered Yorkists were surrounded and slaughtered. York himself was one of the first to die. His son Rutland pleaded to Lord Clifford to be spared, but Clifford, whose father had died at Saint Albans, shouted, "By God's blood, thy father slew mine, and so will I do thee," and stabbed Rutland to death.[28]

The victorious Margaret was now "drunk on the stench of blood and gunpowder and the harsh taste of vengeance."[29] When Clifford brought her the head of the duke of York, she slapped it in the face. She ordered Salisbury, who had been taken prisoner, to be beheaded, as well. Returning to the city of York, she had the heads of York, Salisbury, and Rutland stuck on poles atop the city gate. She mockingly placed a paper crown on York's head. She had two more poles put in place. These, she said, were for Warwick and for York's surviving son, Edward.

Ten years after he had returned from Ireland to challenge Margaret, Richard of York was dead. Margaret had won, but she knew it was not the final victory. Both Warwick and Edward of March would seek their own revenge, and the Wars of the Roses would continue.

3 "This Sun of York"

With the death of Richard at Wakefield, his son Edward of March was now—at the age of nineteen—duke of York and head of the Yorkist cause. Up to this time he had been in the shadow of his father and Warwick, his uncle. He would soon prove himself to be a general superior to both of them, and his victories would all but extinguish the hopes of the house of Lancaster.

Edward had been in northern Wales trying to raise troops when he learned of his father's defeat and death. He also learned that Jasper Tudor, the Lancastrian earl of Pembroke, had landed in south Wales with a mixed force of Irish and French soldiers, recruited to fight for Margaret.

Edward lost no time demonstrating why he has been called "the most consistently successful commander to emerge from the Wars of the Roses."[30] He quickly recruited an army and sought to head off Tudor before he could join forces with Margaret. Showing remarkable speed and mobility, he headed south and overtook Tudor near the town of Mortimer's Cross on February 1, 1461.

On the morning before the battle, because of some unexplained atmospheric phenomenon, it appeared as if there were three suns in the sky. His soldiers were afraid, but Edward calmed them, saying,

"This is a good sign, for these three signs betoken the Father, the Son, and the Holy Ghost. And therefore let us have a good heart, and in the name of Almighty God go we against our enemies."[31] The Battle of Mortimer's Cross was a complete victory

Following his father's death, Edward of March inherited the title duke of York and became the leader of the Yorkist cause.

for Edward. Jasper Tudor escaped, but more than three thousand of his men were killed and many others taken prisoner.

Meanwhile, the victorious Margaret was advancing on London. She had not been able to pay her soldiers and was unable to stop them from looting and burning farms and villages as they marched. The Londoners were terrified, but Warwick, who had remained in London, was strangely inactive. His biographer, Paul Murray Kendall, wrote:

> He stayed in London, permitting the Queen's forces to gobble up the manpower and the resources of the heart of England. . . . Something had gone amiss. The industry, the ebullience [vitality] . . . faltered in the face of a larger and more complex situation. . . . He grasped for shadows, fouling the impetus [momentum] of popular enthusiasm and letting time—of which he had hitherto [until now] been the master—slip away from him.[32]

Warwick Advances

It was not until he heard about Edward's success at Mortimer's Cross that Warwick formed an army and headed north, taking King Henry with him. By this time Margaret's increasingly savage troops were only a week away. Warwick, usually one to attack at once, chose this time to take a defensive position. He left a small force in Saint Albans, where the first battle of the war had been fought six years before, and moved northeast, digging in near the village of Sandridge and blocking the roads from the north.

Margaret outmaneuvered Warwick. Instead of coming down the main road, her army swung west, attacked Saint Albans from the northwest, overwhelmed the Yorkists there, and on February 16 attacked the main body of Warwick's army from the side.

Warwick frantically tried to swing his army around to meet the attack. For a moment it seemed he might succeed. Then, as happened so often in the Wars of the Roses, an act of treachery decided the battle. One of Warwick's captains, Lovelace, suddenly led his troops over to the Lancastrians, and Margaret's soldiers poured through the gap left by the turncoats.

Soon the battlefield was a disorderly jumble of struggling men locked in hand-to-hand combat. The battles of the Wars of the Roses were not like those of the Hundred Years' War. In those earlier battles the tactics of the English and French had been different from each other. The French had relied on mounted knights, and the English on their archers, with the archers having an advantage. During the Wars of the Roses both sides used the same tactics, so the issue was usually settled when the two sides, having used all their arrows, hacked and stabbed at one another with swords, spears, and clubs. As one historian wrote, "nearly all the battles . . . were essentially slugging matches."[33]

Warwick's army, badly outnumbered, soon fell apart. As night came, Warwick was able to rally a few troops and escape, but the rest were killed or taken prisoner. Warwick and what was left of his army headed west to join Edward.

Two of the prisoners were Lord Bonville and Sir Thomas Tyrell. They had been given the job of guarding King Henry, who had spent the battle laughing

During the Hundred Years' War, battles were fought primarily between mounted knights (front and left) and archers (right). During the Wars of the Roses, both sides used the same tactics and were more equally matched.

and singing to himself under a tree out of harm's way. Henry had promised them that if their side lost the battle, they would not be harmed. But Henry had not reckoned on his bloodthirsty wife.

A Cruel Sentence

When the two prisoners were brought before Margaret, she turned to her son, Edward, and asked, "Fair son, with what death shall these two knights die whom you see there?"

"Their heads should be cut off," replied the seven-year-old prince immediately.

As he was led away to his death, Tyrell said, "May the wrath of God fall on those who have taught a child to speak such words."[34]

Margaret now sent word to London that she meant no harm to the city. She asked that she and Henry be admitted in peace. The Londoners, however, feared that Margaret's wild northern troops would destroy the city. They refused to open their gates. Margaret knew that if she attacked London, she would hurt her own cause. She wanted to enter the city as the rightful queen, not as a conqueror. Also, she knew that Edward, the new duke of York, was advancing from the west. Margaret decided to withdraw and led her army back north.

On February 27 Edward's army reached London, which greeted him as a savior. Londoners, especially the wealthy merchants, were tired of constant strife. They had disliked Margaret from the beginning because of her French sympathies. They were weary of the lackluster Henry. They wanted a strong king who would bring order and thought they had found one in Edward—tall, strong, handsome, a proven warrior. As William Shakespeare put it in the famous opening lines to his play *Richard III*, "Now is the winter of our discontent made glorious summer by this sun of York."[35]

Warwick urged Edward to claim the throne. Edward did not require much urging. Unlike his father, Richard, who had hesitated at key moments and let Queen Margaret regain power, Edward seized the opportunity with both hands. On March 1 George Neville, bishop of Exeter and Warwick's younger brother

> caused to be mustered [gathered] his people in St. John's Field, where unto that host were proclaimed and shewed [shown] certain articles and points that King Henry had offended in, whereupon it was demanded of the said people whether the said Henry were worthy to reign as king any longer or no. Whereunto the people

cried hugely and said, Nay, Nay. And after it was asked of them whether they would have the Earl of March [Edward] for their king and they cried with one voice, Yea, Yea.[36]

Edward Becomes King

Three days later Edward entered the royal palace at Westminster, just west of London, took his seat on the throne, grasped the scepter, or staff of office, and proclaimed himself Edward IV, king of England, first king of the house of York.

Despite Warwick's recent defeat it seemed to many that this was as much his victory as Edward's. An Italian visitor to England, Bishop Coppini, wrote to his master, the duke of Milan, "Just now, although matters in England have under-

Upon Warwick's urging, Edward, duke of York, claimed the English throne in March 1461. He assumed the title Edward IV, becoming the first king of the house of York.

gone several fluctuations, yet in the end my lord of Warwick has come off the best and has made a new king of the son of the Duke of York."[37] Thus Warwick earned the nickname by which he is known to history—Kingmaker.

Edward knew he could not truly count himself king until the Lancastrians were defeated. Warwick encouraged him to take advantage of his popularity to raise an army and pursue Margaret. The queen had retreated all the way to Yorkshire and

An Army Run Wild

After the Battle of Wakefield in 1460, Queen Margaret led her victorious troops toward London. She was unable to prevent her soldiers, many of whom were from the remote parts of northern England, from ravaging the countryside and eventually retreated. This account by the prior, or superior, of Croyland Abbey shows the fear felt by the people in the path of Margaret's troops. This extract is from The Wars of the Roses *by J. R. Lander.*

"The duke [Richard of York] being thus removed from this world, the northmen, being sensible [knowing] that the only impediment [barrier] was now withdrawn, and that there was no one now who would care to resist their inroads, again swept onwards like a whirlwind from the north, and in the impulse of their fury attempted to overrun the whole of England. At this period too, fancying that every thing tended to insure them freedom from molestation, paupers and beggars flocked forth from those quarters in infinite numbers, just like so many mice rushing forth from their holes, and universally devoted themselves to spoil and rapine [plunder], without regard of place or person. For besides the vast quantities of property which they collected outside, they also irreverently rushed, in their unbridled and frantic rage, into churches and the other sanctuaries of God, and most nefariously [evilly] plundered them of their chalices, books, and vestments, and, unutterable crime! broke open the pixes [silver boxes] in which were kept the body of Christ [communion wafers] and shook out the sacred elements therefrom. When the priests and the other faithful of Christ in any way offered to make resistance, like so many abandoned wretches as they were, they cruelly slaughtered them in the very churches or church yards. Thus did they proceed with impunity [freedom from punishment], spreading in vast multitudes over a space of thirty miles in breadth, and, covering the whole surface of the earth just like so many locusts, made their way almost to the very walls of London."

was slowly heading toward Scotland. Edward acted swiftly. Only three days after proclaiming himself king, he and Warwick set out from London. They traveled in short marches, allowing recruits to join their army, which swelled to about fifteen thousand. Edward caught Margaret's army near the village of Towton, a few miles south of the city of York.

The Battle of Towton

The Lancastrians, numbering about twenty thousand, had established a fortified position a few miles north of the River Aire and had destroyed a bridge behind them. On February 27 Warwick led a small force to repair the bridge and established a camp on the northern bank, hoping to hold the bridge so that the main body of troops could cross. A Lancastrian detachment commanded by Lord Clifford—the same man who had killed Edward's brother Edmund at Wakefield—suddenly attacked. Warwick was wounded in the leg by an arrow, and the Yorkists had to retreat across the Aire.

Edward countered by quickly sending Warwick's uncle, Lord Fauconberg, four miles upriver to an undefended crossing. Clifford thought he had defeated Edward's advance scouts and that the main body of the army was far to the south. He was taken completely by surprise when Fauconberg attacked from the east, and Edward, from the south. After three hours of furious fighting, the Yorkists triumphed. Lord Clifford was dead. He had paused during the battle, taking his helmet off to get some air. At that moment a Yorkist arrow hit him in the throat.

With the bridge now firmly held, Edward moved all his troops across the Aire. The next day was March 29, Palm Sunday. Edward arranged his army in a battle line along a ridge. Across a valley, on another ridge with their right wing protected by a stream known as Cock Beck, were the soldiers of Queen Margaret commanded by Henry Percy, earl of Northumberland, and Henry Beaufort, duke of Somerset. Both sides knew that with the two rivals for the throne facing one another, the battle would be decisive. Virtually every noble family in England was represented. In addition to King Edward, four dukes, six earls, and twenty barons were present. King Henry, however, was not there. He had

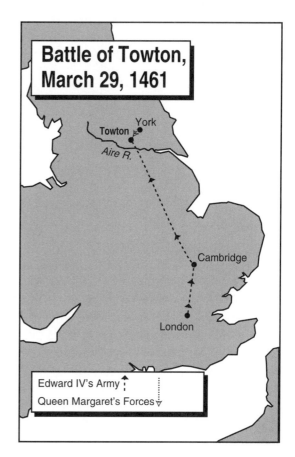

Battle of Towton, March 29, 1461

Towton · York
Aire R.
Cambridge
London

Edward IV's Army
Queen Margaret's Forces

Heavy snowfall greatly hindered the efforts of the royal army during the Battle of Towton on March 29, 1461.

objected to a battle's being fought on a holy day and had remained in York to pray. Margaret and her son also had stayed behind.

Edward rode up and down the line of battle, showing himself to his troops. He said that anyone who was afraid was free to leave, but that once the battle started, any man who turned and ran could be killed by one of his own men and the killer would be rewarded. To show his own determination, he sprang from his horse and stabbed it to death. He would remain, he said, to live or die with his men.

As the armies faced one another, it began to snow heavily. The south wind whipped the snow into the eyes of the sol-diers of Lancaster. Seeing his opportunity, Edward ordered the attack. His left wing, under Fauconberg, advanced, and archers poured volleys of arrows into the Lancastrians. The royal troops tried to reply, but the snow blinded them and the wind made their arrows fall far short.

At last Edward ordered a full charge toward the center of the Lancastrian line. It was beaten back, and the Lancastrians pushed forward. They almost broke through Edward's troops, but Warwick, shouting orders and encouragement, steadied the line.

The Yorkists were outnumbered, how-ever, and slowly fell back. Only the heroics of Warwick and Edward, who seemingly was everywhere, a giant figure in armor, slashing about with a sword and rushing to plug up every weak point in his line, prevented a rout. Still, the Yorkists were forced to retreat and were on the verge of defeat when reinforcements suddenly arrived. The duke of Norfolk and his army of men from Kent appeared out of the snow on the Lancastrians' left. The Yorkist line stiffened, and the battle raged on.

The Battle of Towton

The Battle of Towton, fought on March 29, 1461, was the largest and bloodiest of the Wars of the Roses. This account is from a letter written by the earl of Warwick's brother George, later archbishop of York, to Francesco Coppini, an ambassador from the pope in Rome. The account is quoted from J. R. Lander's The Wars of the Roses.

"That day there was a great conflict, which began with the rising of the sun, and lasted until the tenth hour of the night, so great was the pertinacity [refusal to yield] and boldness of the men, who never heeded the possibility of a miserable death. Of the enemy who fled, great numbers were drowned in a river near the town of Tadcaster, eight miles from York, because they themselves had broken [the] bridge to cut our passage that way, so that none could pass, and a great part of the rest who got away who gathered in the said town and city [Tadcaster], were slain and so many dead bodies were seen as to cover an area six miles long by three broad and about four furlongs [a furlong is 220 yards]. In this battle eleven lords of the enemy fell, including the earl of Devon, the earl of Northumberland, Lord Clifford and Neville with some cavaliers; and from what we hear from persons worthy of confidence, some 28,000 persons perished on one side and the other. O miserable and luckless race and powerful people, would you have no spark of pity for our own blood, of which we have lost so much of fine quality by the civil war, even if you had no compassion for the French! If it had been fought under some capable and experienced captain against the Turks, the enemies of the Christian name, it would have been a great stroke and blow. But to tell the truth, owing to these civil discords, our riches are beginning to give out, and we are shedding our own blood copiously [abundantly] among ourselves."

England's Bloodiest Battle

The Battle of Towton was the longest and bloodiest battle ever fought on English soil. It lasted ten hours, but the Lancastrians finally were pushed back, broke ranks, and ran. Screaming, the Yorkists pursued their enemies toward Cock Beck. Some Lancastrians were able to crowd across a small bridge. Hundreds tried to cross the stream, now flooded, and were drowned in their heavy armor. The River Aire ran red with blood, and the snow was stained a bright red, as well.

More than ten thousand men had been killed, including Henry Percy and Andrew Trollope, the same man who had deserted Warwick at Ludlow in 1459. Somerset managed to escape and make his way to York. There he met Henry, Margaret, and Prince Edward, and all fled north to Scotland. King Edward entered York in triumph. One of his first acts was to have the heads of his father and brother and Warwick's father taken down from above the gate, replacing them with heads of executed Lancastrian nobles.

From York, Edward moved north. The Percy stronghold of Durham in Northumberland surrendered to him, and he forced many local nobles to swear allegiance. Then he made a leisurely return to London while Warwick and his brother, Lord

Lasting ten hours, the Battle of Towton was the longest and bloodiest battle ever fought on English soil. Hundreds of Lancastrian soldiers drowned while trying to escape the Yorkists.

King Louis XI of France agreed to help Queen Margaret regain control of England in exchange for possession of Calais.

called Henry VI, from the occupation, usurpation [wrongful assumption], reign and governance of the same realm of England."[38] Acts of attainder [confiscation of property] were passed against 113 Lancastrians, including Henry, Margaret, and their son, Edward. Jasper Tudor was attainted, and his title, earl of Pembroke, was given to a Yorkist noble, Lord Herbert. Along with his new title, Herbert gained control of the former earl's four-year-old nephew, Henry Tudor, earl of Richmond. Many years later it would be Henry, son of Jasper's dead brother, Edmund, and his wife, Margaret Beaufort, the daughter of John Beaufort, who would finally emerge as the lone winner in the Wars of the Roses.

Former queen Margaret, meanwhile, was not idle. She now sought help from both Scotland and France and was willing to give away anything to get it. To Scotland she promised the border city of Berwick-upon-Tweed. She went to France to visit the new king, Louis XI, and agreed that Calais would be the price of his help.

Margaret Returns

In November 1462 Margaret returned from France to Scotland with a small army of French soldiers. Despite the oaths recently sworn to Edward, most of northern England remained loyal to Henry. The three strongest castles—Bamburgh, Alnwick, and Dunstanburgh—quickly went over to Margaret's side.

Once more Edward reacted with speed. Five days after the castles surrendered, he was on his way north to join Warwick, who had been busy in Yorkshire recruiting soldiers. Soon all three castles

Montagu, remained in the north to guard against an attack from Scotland or an uprising of those loyal to the Lancasters.

Edward reached London in June and was formally crowned on the twenty-eighth. As part of the festivities Edward's younger brothers received titles. George became duke of Clarence, and nine-year-old Richard was made duke of Gloucester. Richard had been a sickly child, born with one shoulder higher than the other. Many years later his death would bring the Wars of the Roses to an end.

Parliament met and affirmed Edward's right to the throne, removing "Henry, late were under attack. Margaret, who was at Bamburgh, saw that the odds against her were too great. Along with her son, she fled in a small ship. A fierce storm arose, and the ship began to sink. Margaret's party was able to transfer to a fishing boat, but their first ship sank, along with all of Margaret's baggage and treasure. She eventually made her way back to Scotland.

Edward IV thought he had seen the last of Margaret. He wanted to make peace. Therefore, he pardoned both Somerset and Ralph Percy, the new earl of Northumberland, both of whom swore an oath of allegiance to him and were restored to their lands. Margaret, however, would never accept defeat. Back in Scotland, she raised an army of two thousand Scots and Frenchmen and invaded England once more, this time bringing King Henry and Prince Edward. Percy quickly went back to her side, and soon all three northern fortresses were back in Lancastrian hands.

In June, Margaret received a severe blow when a fleet of French ships bringing supplies and men was captured. Then, on July 10, 1463, her Scots troops deserted. Once more Margaret fled with her husband and son. After many hardships—at one point they had only one herring and a single loaf of bread to last five days—she reached France with her son, having left Henry in Scotland. She was to remain in France seven years, never ceasing in her effort to win back the throne of England for her son.

Yorkist Triumph

Without Margaret to inspire them, the Lancastrians in England faltered. Edward IV reached a truce with the king of France and the duke of Burgundy, from whom Margaret had been seeking help. Then he set out to eliminate the remaining Lancastrian strongholds. He suffered a setback when Somerset once more changed sides, but on April 25, 1464, Warwick's brother, Lord Montagu, won a battle at Hedgeley Moor, at which Ralph Percy was killed.

Now only Somerset remained to fight for King Henry. He rounded up every loyal Lancastrian soldier he could find and met Montagu's army near the northern city of Hexham. On May 15 Somerset was overwhelmed, taken prisoner, and shown no mercy. A master cook used his cleaver to knock off Somerset's spurs, a sign of stripping him of knighthood. His coat of arms was torn from his clothing. He was paraded through the streets of Hexham and beheaded.

It was a moment of supreme triumph for the house of York. Meanwhile, poor Henry VI had been left on his own. He wandered around northern England and in 1465 was captured and delivered to Edward to be sent to the Tower of London. Margaret and her son were impoverished fugitives in France, and virtually all Lancastrian opposition was dead or exiled. Margaret still burned for revenge, but it seemed as if only a miracle could restore her cause.

4 The Kingmaker

The Lancastrian defeat at Hexham in 1464 and Queen Margaret's flight to France should have ended the Wars of the Roses. Within six years, however, the house of Lancaster was restored to power. Amazingly, it was with the help of the man who had been the chief cause of the Yorkist triumph—Richard Neville, earl of Warwick.

After his father's death at the Battle of Wakefield in 1460, Warwick became the richest man in England. His income from the combined estates of Westmorland, Salisbury, and Warwick exceeded even that of King Edward. His brother George was archbishop of York and chancellor of England. Another brother, Lord Montagu, was made earl of Northumberland. His uncle, Lord Fauconberg, was created earl of Kent.

Elsewhere in Europe some people thought Warwick actually was the king. King Louis XI of France once joked, "They tell me that they have two rulers in England—Monsieur le Warwick and another whose name I have forgotten."[39] Indeed, Warwick sometimes lived like a king. In 1466, when Edward entertained some visitors with a fifty-course dinner, Warwick felt compelled to give them a sixty-course dinner the following week.

Power was everything to Warwick. He did not yearn for new titles. He was con-

tent to remain an earl when others received the loftier title of duke as long as he remained the most powerful man in England. He did not wish to become king, but he wanted to dominate Edward IV, much as Margaret had dominated Henry VI. Edward, however, was no meek, timid

Richard Neville, earl of Warwick, was the richest and most powerful man in England—often more powerful than King Edward IV.

Henry. As he grew older, he made it clear that he would not be governed by anyone. As Ross wrote, "The main reason for the renewal of civil war in 1469 was Warwick's arrogant refusal to accept a subordinate [lower] role."[40]

At first Edward was content to let Warwick oversee most of the military and diplomatic affairs of England. Edward, in 1464, was twenty-two years old and had been at war with the Lancastrians since he was fifteen. Now, with victory seemingly assured, he wanted to enjoy himself. He did not ignore affairs of state, but he much preferred hunting, feasting, tournaments, good food and wine, and—above all—the company of beautiful women. The royal court became a more fashionable place.

The serious, sober Warwick wanted Edward to marry, settle down, and produce a son to inherit the throne. Presently the next in line was Edward's younger brother Gloucester, who was handsome and strong but also arrogant, irresponsible, and vain. Warwick also wanted to forge an alliance with France to head off any possible attempt by Louis XI to put Henry and Margaret back in power.

The French Match

Warwick saw a way to accomplish both objectives at once by arranging a marriage between Edward and a bride from the French royal house. This also suited the king of France, since England would be allied with France instead of with France's enemy, Burgundy. Louis XI proposed to Warwick that Edward marry his sister-in-law, Bona of Savoy, a region in southeastern France. In July 1464 Warwick went to France to work out an agreement. Edward agreed that he should go but refused to commit himself to the marriage.

Negotiations went on throughout the summer. Edward raised one objection after another. Finally, at a meeting of the royal council in September, Warwick demanded to know Edward's thoughts on marriage. Edward replied that he wanted to be married, but "perchance our choice may not be to the liking of everyone present."[41] The council thought he was joking and someone asked whom, then, would he like to marry? Then Edward stunned his councilors. He was already married, he calmly told them.

Three years earlier, as he returned to London from the Battle of Towton, Edward had paused for a time at the village of Stony Stratford. The story goes that he was hunting in the woods nearby when he saw a beautiful woman holding two small boys by the hand. She knelt by his horse, looked up, and tearfully begged him to have mercy on her family.

The woman was Elizabeth Woodville, daughter of Jacquetta, the widow of the duke of Bedford, and her second husband, the upstart Richard Woodville, Lord Rivers. The family had been solid supporters of the Lancasters. It had been Rivers who had been given the task of capturing Warwick in Calais, only to be captured himself. Elizabeth's husband, Lancastrian knight John Grey, had been killed at the Second Battle of Saint Albans and left her with two small sons.

Edward was overwhelmed by Elizabeth's beauty. Sixteenth-century historian Raphael Holinshed described her as

both of such beauty and favor that with her sober demeanor, sweet looks, and

On May 1, 1464, King Edward IV secretly wed Elizabeth Woodville (pictured), a young Lancastrian widow.

comely smiling (neither too wanton, nor too bashful), besides her pleasant tongue and trim wit, she so allured and made subject unto her the heart of that great prince [Edward] that . . . he finally resolved himself to marry her.[42]

At first Edward's intention was not to marry Elizabeth but to add her to his growing list of mistresses. Elizabeth, however, refused to submit to the king's advances. It was marriage or nothing.

The Secret Marriage

Finally Edward gave in. In April 1464 he went to Stony Stratford, told his men he was going hunting, and rode alone to Grafton, the home of Elizabeth's mother.

There, on May 1, he and Elizabeth were married. The only witnesses were Jacquetta, two of her serving women, the priest, and a choirboy. Over the next five months Edward frequently hunted in the vicinity of Grafton and sneaked away to join his bride whenever possible.

When Edward was finally forced to admit his marriage, his council was shocked. Elizabeth, they said, was totally unsuitable. She was five years older than Edward. She came from a Lancastrian family, and her father was nothing more than a former attendant to Henry VI's father.

No one was more angry than Warwick. For months he had been negotiating a French marriage for Edward. Now he had been made to look like a fool in front of all Europe. Warwick swallowed his anger, however, and, accompanied by Edward's brother Clarence, escorted his new queen to court.

The split between Edward and Warwick became greater when the king began to shower titles and riches on Elizabeth's family—and a big family it was. In addition to her two sons, the queen had a father, five brothers, and seven sisters. Edward took care of all of them. Her father was made an earl. Her sisters were married to dukes and earls. Her brother Anthony was made Lord Scales. Another brother became a bishop. Yet another brother, John, was married to the wealthy widow of the duke of Norfolk, although he was twenty and she was almost eighty.

People thought King Edward did all this out of love for Elizabeth. Actually, he was far shrewder than that. By advancing so many of Elizabeth's relatives, he was forming a core of support that would be loyal to him, not to the powerful Warwick and the Nevilles.

The Treachery of Clarence

In an effort to end Warwick's domination, King Edward IV (pictured) began gathering supporters who would be loyal to him rather than the powerful earl.

Warwick had not given up on an alliance with France. If Edward was no longer available for a French marriage, there was Edward's sister Margaret. In 1467 Warwick and Louis XI reached an agreement whereby Margaret would marry a French prince, and Edward's youngest brother, Richard of Gloucester, would marry Louis's daughter. When Warwick took the agreement back to England, however, he found that Edward had been negotiating, as well, and had agreed to a marriage between Margaret and the duke of Burgundy, Louis XI's great rival.

Warwick was furious. Once more Edward had made him look ridiculous. Now the powerful earl tried another avenue. He began to make approaches to Edward's brother George of Clarence. Since Edward and Elizabeth had no sons together, Clarence was next in line for the throne. Warwick, wishing to regain his hold on the throne, proposed that Clarence become his son-in-law by marrying his oldest daughter, Isobel of Warwick. Edward refused to give his permission. Warwick defied the king and in 1469 took Clarence and Isobel to Calais, where Warwick was still captain, and had the couple married by his brother, the archbishop. Warwick's plan was a bold one: to remove Edward from the throne and replace him with Clarence.

Warwick's agents began spreading rumors throughout England that Edward was illegitimate and that Clarence was the true heir of Richard of York. A rebellion broke out in Yorkshire, led by a person calling himself Robin of Redesdale, but who actually was Sir John Conyers, a relative of Warwick. As the rebels headed south, Edward marched north with only a few soldiers, calling on the earl of Devon and the earl of Pembroke to bring their troops from the west.

In July 1469 Edward reached Nottingham and waited for his reinforcements to arrive. Meanwhile, Warwick and Clarence crossed the English Channel with an army. Landing in Kent, they proclaimed that they were loyal subjects of Edward and had come only to overthrow the king's evil councilors—the Woodvilles. Many of the nobles in southern England, envious of all that had been given to the Woodvilles, joined them.

Edward now realized the danger. His only chance was to join with Devon and Pembroke, but the two earls were intercepted and defeated by Conyers at the Battle of Edgecote on July 26. Both Devon and Pembroke were executed. Edward tried to send his wife's father and brother, Lord Rivers and Sir John Woodville, to safety, but they were captured and beheaded.

Edward was trapped. Warwick sent a small force under his brother, Archbishop Neville, to the village of Olney to seize the king. The archbishop arrived at midnight and demanded that Edward accompany him. Edward told him to come back the next day. "Get up at once and come to my brother, Warwick, without

A Secret Marriage

In 1464, even as the earl of Warwick was negotiating a marriage between King Edward IV and a member of the French royal family, Edward was married in secret to Elizabeth Woodville, widow of a Lancastrian knight. Chronicler Robert Fabyan told this story, which is found in The Wars of the Roses *by J. R. Lander.*

"In such pass time, in most secret manner, upon the first day of May, King Edward spoused Elizabeth, late the wife of Sir John Grey, knight, which before time was slain at Towton or York field [sic], which spousals [nuptials] were solemnised early in the morning at a town named Grafton, near Stony Stratford; at which marriage was no persons present but the spous [groom], the spousess [bride], the duchess of Bedford her mother, the priest, two gentlewomen, and a young man to help the priest sing. After which spousals ended, he [Edward] went to bed, and so tarried there upon three or four hours, and after departed and rode again to Stony Stratford, and came in manner as though he had been on hunting, and there went to bed again. And within a day or two after, he sent to Grafton, to the Lord Ryvers [Rivers] father unto his wife, shewing to him that he would come and lodge with him a certain season, where he was received with all honour, and so tarried there by the space of four days. In which season, she [Elizabeth] nightly to his bed was brought, in so secret manner that almost none but her mother was of counsel. And so this marriage was a season kept secret after, till needly it must be discovered and disclosed by mean of other [another marriage] which were offered unto the king."

further argument," the archbishop commanded his king.[43] Edward knew resistance was useless and thus became a prisoner in his own land.

The King Is Freed

Edward was taken to Warwick's castle at Middleham, north of York. Warwick was now master of England, although he claimed to be ruling in Edward's name. Many English nobles, however, did not trust the great earl. They knew he had his own self-interest at heart. When a revolt broke out in the north by forces still loyal to the house of Lancaster, Warwick summoned troops to put it down. His orders were ignored. The Yorkist nobles refused to cooperate unless Edward was set free. Warwick was forced to admit he could not govern the kingdom and gave Edward his liberty.

Edward was still in a dangerous position. His brother Richard of Gloucester and his good friend William, Lord Hastings, raised an army to help him, but the

---

Warwick's Alliance with Clarence

The earl of Warwick, frustrated in his efforts to dominate the young King Edward IV, made an alliance with Edward's younger brother, the duke of Clarence. The scene was recorded by chronicler Jehan de Waurin and is found in A. R. Myers's English Historical Documents.

"While the king [Edward IV] was at Windsor, and the French [ambassadors] were in London, there came the Duke of Clarence, and had a talk with the Earl of Warwick, on the matter of the embassy, and how the ambassadors were grumbling because the king had shown them so little welcome. Then the Duke of Clarence replied that it was not his fault, and the Earl said he knew that very well. They spoke of the circle round the king, saying that he had scarcely any of the blood royal at court, and that Lord Rivers and his family dominated everything. And when they had discussed this matter, the duke asked the earl how they could remedy this. Then the Earl of Warwick replied that if the duke would trust him, he would make him king of England, or governor of the whole realm, and he need be in no doubt that most of the country would support him. When the Duke of Clarence, who was young and trusting, heard the earl promise so much to him, together with the hand of the earl's elder daughter in marriage, he agreed, on these promises that the earl made to him, to take her as his wife."

When Warwick switched over to the Lancastrian faction, he realized the importance of having Queen Margaret (pictured) as his ally. With her help, Warwick planned to overthrow King Edward IV.

by Edward on March 12. As they fled, they threw away their heavy jackets so as to run faster, giving the battle its name: Losecoat Field.

Papers captured from the rebels showed that Warwick and Clarence had been behind the revolt. When Edward, now more secure, marched against them, they fled. The city of Calais, now loyal to Edward, would not admit them, and in May they finally took refuge elsewhere in France. They were welcomed by the crafty Louis XI, who wanted to use them to turn England away from its alliance with Burgundy.

Louis welcomed Warwick as if he were visiting royalty. He praised Warwick's abilities and said that together they could rule western Europe. By mid-June their plans were set. Louis would provide troops for Warwick to help him overthrow Edward and put Henry VI back on the throne. Henry's son, Edward, would be married to Warwick's younger daughter, Anne. Clarence had to be satisfied with a vague promise that he would inherit the throne if no heir was born to Edward and Anne. And once Warwick controlled England, he would join with Louis to conquer Burgundy.

king did not feel strong enough to challenge Warwick directly. Instead, he behaved as though all was forgiven—but it was not. A letter written at the time reported that "the king himself hath good language [speaks well] of the Lords of Clarence, of Warwick, and of my Lords of York [Archbishop Neville] and Oxford, saying they be his best friends . . . but his household men have other languages."[44]

Edward slowly but surely rebuilt his support, which had been severely damaged by the Battle of Edgecote. The next time Warwick and Clarence tried to spark a rebellion, the king was ready. An uprising early in 1470 was stopped almost before it started. An army of rebels attempting to march south to join Warwick was defeated

Margaret in Poverty

The difficulty, both Warwick and Louis knew, was to get Queen Margaret to agree to an alliance with her old enemy. Margaret had been living on a meager allowance given to her by her father, René. She and her small band of faithful Lancastrians existed in near poverty. One of her followers wrote, "We be all in great poverty,

The King Is Captured

In 1469 the forces of the earl of Warwick and the duke of Clarence trapped Edward IV in a village near Coventry. The chronicle of Jehan de Waurin, this excerpt of which is found in English Historical Documents, *edited by A. R. Myers, tells how he was taken prisoner.*

"About midnight there came to the king the Archbishop of York, accompanied by many men of war, and thrust himself into the king's lodgings, saying to the king's bodyguard that he must speak to the king . . . but the king sent answer that he was resting and would come in the morning, when he would gladly hear him. But the archbishop was not satisfied with this reply, and sent renewed messages to say that it was essential for him to speak to the king . . . and then the king commanded them to let him come [to] him to hear what he said, for they had no suspicion of him. When the archbishop came into the room, where he found the king in bed, he said to him brusquely: 'Sire, get up!', whereupon the king asked to be excused, saying that he had not yet had any rest: but the archbishop, false and disloyal as he was, said to him the second time: 'You must get up and come to my brother Warwick, for you cannot oppose this.' And then the king, for fear that worse might befall, dressed himself and the archbishop brought him quietly to the place where the said earl and Clarence were between Warwick and Coventry, where he presented to them his king and sovereign lord, taken by him in the manner aforesaid. The Earl of Warwick greeted the king courteously without doing him any bodily harm; but to keep his person safe Edward was sent to Warwick Castle, and they provided him there with guards, who led him every day to take exercise where he wished, to the limit of one league or two."

but yet the Queen sustaineth us in meat and drink, so as we be not in extreme necessity. Her highness may do not more to [for] us than she doth."[45]

When Louis explained his plan to her, Margaret was furious. Under no circumstances, she said, could she ever forgive Warwick—the man who had removed her husband from his throne, killed many of her friends, and forced her and her son into exile. She remained opposed despite the efforts of both Louis and René. At last, when her own followers advised her that this was the only chance to restore the house of Lancaster, she agreed to at least meet Warwick.

On July 22 Warwick was taken by Louis into a chamber where Margaret was seated, Prince Edward at her side. Warwick went on his knees before the queen, conceded the wrongs he had done her, and begged her forgiveness. A witness wrote that Warwick, after acknowledging his part in the overthrow of Henry VI by Edward IV, "now, seeing the evil turns that the king [Edward IV] hath kept him . . . will be as far contrary and enemy unto him hereafter."[46]

The earl spoke for fifteen minutes, while Margaret watched in cold silence. When she finally spoke, it was to unleash a rain of curses on Warwick, calling him faithless and cowardly. Warwick listened with bowed head. At last, having expressed the anger built up over years, Margaret allowed Warwick to rise and formally, though not warmly, forgave her former foe.

Warwick summoned from England all the troops loyal to him. Louis provided more troops and the ships to carry them all back across the channel. By September everything was ready, and on the twelfth the Lancastrians, led by Warwick and Clarence, landed in Sandwich and Plymouth on the southern coast of England. Margaret and Prince Edward remained in France, hoping to cross over once victory was secured.

A Warning Ignored

King Edward was in the northern part of England, dealing with a minor uprising, when the landing took place. In fact that revolt had probably been organized by Warwick to get Edward out of his capital. Edward had been warned by the duke of Burgundy that the invasion was to take place but had not taken the warning seriously. Now he ordered Lord Montagu, Warwick's brother, to march south from his estates near the border with Scotland.

Montagu had remained loyal to Edward throughout Warwick's earlier grab for power. Edward had rewarded him by naming him earl of Northumberland. Later, however, Edward needed help from the powerful Percy family and restored the Northumberland earldom to them. Now Montagu, outwardly loyal to Edward, had secretly been in communication with his brother. He marched south at the head of a large army as if he were going to join Edward. When he was nine miles from Edward's camp, where Edward was staying, he announced his intention to fight on Warwick's side. Montagu's men responded by cheering for King Henry.

The rebels wanted to capture King Edward, as one chronicle related:

> But anon [immediately] one of the host went out from the fellowship [Montagu's army], and told King Edward all manner of thing, and bade him avoid, for he was not strong enough to give battle to Marquess Montagu; and then anon King Edward hastened [himself] in all that he might to the town of Lynn, and there he took shipping one Michelmas day [September 29], in the tenth year of his reign . . . and sailed over the sea into Flanders, to his brother-in-law the duke of Burgundy, for succour [relief] and help.[47]

Edward was accompanied by only a few companions, including his brother

Richard and Lord Hastings. The king had been able to escape with little more than the clothes he wore. When he arrived in Flanders, an area north of France that was part of Burgundy, he had only one thing of value to offer the captain of his ship—his fur-lined cloak. A French diplomat there wrote:

> Strange it was to see this poor king . . . to fly after this sort [to flee in this way] pursued by his own servants, and the rather, for that he had by the space of twelve or thirteen years lived in greater pleasures and delicacies

than any prince in his time: for he had wholly given himself to dames, hunting, hawking, and banqueting.[48]

An Untidy King

On October 6 Archbishop Neville went to the Tower of London to release Henry VI. He was found in a gloomy room with only a dog and a caged bird for company and "not worshipfully arrayed [dressed] as a prince, and not so cleanly kept as such a Prince should be."[49] The next day the be-

Henry VI was imprisoned in the Tower of London (pictured) during the reign of Edward IV. He was released on October 6, 1470, after spending nearly five years in the ancient fortress.

Warwick's Apology to Margaret

In 1470 King Louis XI of France brought about a reconciliation between the earl of Warwick and Queen Margaret, who had been the bitterest of enemies. This description of Warwick's apology and defense was written by an anonymous French observer. It is included in The Wars of the Roses, *by J. R. Lander.*

"Th' earl of Warwick, all these things [Margaret's complaints against him] heard, said unto the queen that he confessed well that by his conduct and mean [manner] the King Henry and she were put out of the realm of England; but for an excuse and justification thereof, he shewed that the King Henry and she by their false counsel had enterprised [initiated] the destruction of him and his friends in body and in goods, which he never had deserved against them. And him [Warwick] seemed that for such causes, and the great evil will that they have showed him he had a rightwise cause to labour their undoing and destruction, and that therein he had not done but that a nobleman outrayed and disperred [outraged and disparaged] ought to have done. Also he said over that, and well confessed that he was causer of the [creation] of the king of England that now is [Edward IV], but now, seeing the evil terms that the king hath kept him, and cast him out of the realm, and, as much as he hath been with him in times passed, now he will be as far contrary and enemy unto him hereafter; beseeching there the queen and the said prince [Margaret's son, Edward] that so they would take and repute [believe] him, and forgive him that in time passed he had done and attempted against them: offering himself to be bounden, by all manner wise, to be their true and faithful subject in time to come."

wildered Henry, described by one observer as having been hauled from one place to another like a sack of wool, stood in a blue velvet gown once owned by Edward, as Warwick and Clarence rode into London in triumph.

Some of Henry's most faithful supporters soon joined the two leading rebels, among them old Jasper Tudor and his nephew, Henry, now fourteen. Meanwhile Edward IV's pregnant queen and his three daughters had taken refuge in Westminster Abbey. Elizabeth claimed the right of sanctuary, meaning that she could not be seized while in a church. The house of Lancaster was now back in power; but even as the Lancastrians celebrated, the house of York was planning revenge.

Chapter

5 The Last of the Lancasters

When King Edward IV fled to Burgundy in 1470, the earl of Warwick and Queen Margaret once more had the upper hand in the Wars of the Roses. They must have known, however, that their grab for power would not bring lasting peace. Sure enough, before another year had passed, Edward was again challenging them for his throne, and this challenge would settle the fate of the house of Lancaster.

Since his enemies had formed an alliance with France, Edward knew his only chance was an alliance with France's enemy, Burgundy. Duke Charles of Burgundy, however, was hesitant to come out in open support of Edward. He feared that if Edward failed, England and France would unite against Burgundy. He did not yet know that this was already Louis XI's plan.

In England, meanwhile, Parliament met and reversed the past bills of attainder against the Lancastrians while passing new ones against the Yorkists. Margaret's supporters were restored to their old positions, with one notable exception. Warwick, needing the support of the Percy family, did not restore the earldom of Northumberland to his brother, Lord Montagu. Henry VI was present at these meetings but had little idea what was going on. A Burgundian diplomat compared him to "no more than a crowned calf, a shadow on the wall."[50]

Two major Lancastrians were missing. Queen Margaret refused to risk the life of her son, Prince Edward, until she felt the situation completely secure. Warwick pleaded with her to cross the channel to England. He thought she and her son would be able to inspire many of the nobles who were sitting back, waiting to see which side would win. Margaret, however, would not budge.

A Yorkist Heir

In November the situation changed. On November 2 Queen Elizabeth, still in Westminster Abbey, gave birth to a son—another Edward. This birth of a Yorkist heir to the throne was a threat to Margaret, who now decided to return to England. Elizabeth's plight had won the sympathy of the common people, and the new prince served as a hopeful sign to those loyal to his father.

Margaret traveled to Paris in December and then to the city of Rouen in Normandy. She would remain there, she said, until Warwick arrived personally in France to escort her to England. Warwick, how-

On November 2, 1470, Queen Elizabeth gave birth to Prince Edward (pictured), the Yorkist heir to the throne. The prince's birth renewed hope that Edward IV would reclaim the monarchy.

ever, was afraid that there might be a rebellion if he left the country. When Margaret, after a delay of several weeks, decided to come in a ship that Warwick sent for her, storms prevented her sailing.

Edward's Invasion

On November 28 England and France publicly announced their treaty to make war on Burgundy. This led Duke Charles to agree to loan King Edward troops and ships with which to try to regain his throne. By February 1471 Edward and his troops were in Flanders, outfitting an invasion fleet. It sailed, with about twelve hundred soldiers aboard, on March 11.

Edward tried to land at Cromer on the eastern coast of England but found that the area had been heavily fortified by Warwick. His ships put out to sea once more and, after being blown here and there by the same storms that were keeping Margaret in France, landed far to the north at Ravenspur on a peninsula in Yorkshire known as Holderness, the same place Henry of Bolingbroke had landed in 1399.

Yorkshire, despite Edward and his father having held the title duke of York, was sympathetic to the Lancastrians, and Edward received a cool welcome. A song of the time described it:

> Lord, the unkyndnes was shewid to Kynge Edward that day!
> At his londynge [landing] in Holdyrness he had grett payne:
> His subjectes and people wolde not hym obey,
> Off him and his people they had grett disdayne,
> There shewid him unkyndnes, and answereid him playne,
> As for kynge he shuld not londe there for well ne wood
> Yett londed that gentill prynce, the will of God was soo.[51]

Edward was careful to adopt the same strategy as had Henry of Bolingbroke and Edward's father, the duke of York, before him. He had not come, he said, for the throne, but merely to claim his rightful inheritance. The city of York decided to admit him only if he left his army outside the walls. Edward agreed and rode into the city with only a few companions, shouting, "Long live Henry and Prince Edward."[52]

Edward and his small army could easily have been defeated at this point by either

In February 1471 Edward IV outfitted an invasion fleet to overthrow Henry VI and recapture the English crown.

Henry Percy, earl of Northumberland, or Lord Montagu. Neither one made a move. Warwick had ordered Montagu to attack, but Montagu later claimed he never got the message. Montagu probably hesitated because he was still angry at Warwick for not making him earl of Northumberland. As for Percy, he stayed out of the conflict, waiting to see who would come out on top.

Edward Reclaims the Crown

As his potential enemies stood still, Edward moved south into an area of the country more loyal to him. His strength increased daily. On March 29, at Sandal Castle, he announced his intention to reclaim the throne.

Warwick decided that the time had come for an all-out attack on Edward. He would advance north from London, Montagu would move in from the north, the duke of Exeter and the earl of Oxford from the east, and the duke of Clarence, Edward's brother, from the west.

Nothing went as Warwick had planned. Clarence was moving too slowly. Montagu hung back, still playing for time. Edward then boldly attacked Exeter and Oxford instead of waiting to be attacked by them. When he came within three miles, the two dukes, thinking he had a huge army, turned and fled.

Warwick and Edmund Beaufort, duke of Somerset, had been marching north with a small army. When Edward learned this, he quickly wheeled his army and headed west to cut them off. Terrified, Warwick and his troops took refuge within the walls of the city of Coventry, hoping Clarence would arrive soon. He did, but the result was hardly to Warwick's liking.

Clarence felt he had been ignored in the agreement between Warwick and the king of France. Now, seeing Edward's success, he decided to switch sides once more. The king and his renegade brother met on the road between Warwick and Banbury. Clarence knelt at Edward's feet. Edward quickly raised him up and embraced him in full view of both armies. All Clarence's troops, supposedly on their way to assist Warwick, now pinned the white rose of York on their jackets.

By now Warwick had been joined at Coventry by Montagu, Oxford, and Exeter. He expected Edward and Clarence to return and give battle. He was wrong. Instead, Edward ignored Warwick and headed south, toward London. Warwick sent word to his brother George, archbishop of York, to keep Edward out of London.

As usual Edward acted too quickly for his enemies. He was only a day's march from London when the archbishop tried to rally the city against him. Poor old Henry VI, the "political vegetable," was brought out for a procession, still wearing Edward's old blue velvet gown, now stained and frayed.[53] If the archbishop thought this would inspire the Londoners, he was mistaken. The sight of Henry, according to one observer, inspired the crowd about as much as "a fire painted on the wall warmed the old woman."[54] The gates of London were thrown open to Edward on Thursday, April 11.

Edward in Triumph

Edward entered the city in triumph. He went to Westminster Abbey, was reunited with Queen Elizabeth, and saw his infant son, Edward, for the first time. He could not stay long. At 4 P.M. the next day he and his army marched north toward a showdown with Warwick. Henry VI, slumping listlessly in his saddle, was taken along. Edward had learned that Margaret had finally sailed from France, and he did not want her to get control of Henry.

Warwick, along with Oxford, Exeter, and Montagu, had finally left Coventry and was heading to meet Edward. He moved through Saint Albans and on Saturday night camped along a ridge a few miles north of the village of Barnet. Warwick sent scouts to discover if Edward had left London. The scouts ran into Edward's army and hurried back to warn the earl.

Edward's army could have spent the night in Barnet, but the king, as usual, did the unexpected. He moved his soldiers silently through the darkness until they were only a few hundred yards from the Lancastrians. Throughout the night Warwick's cannons kept up a steady fire, but the cannonballs sailed harmlessly over the heads of Edward's men, whom he had ordered to remain silent.

The next day, April 14, was Easter Sunday. A dense fog covered the hollow in which Edward's army lay, hiding them from Warwick's troops. Sometime between 5 and 6 A.M., Edward "committed his cause and quarrel to Almighty God, advanced banners, did blow up trumpets, and set upon them."[55] Warwick was surprised. He had thought the Yorkists to be a mile or so away, yet here they were, charging up the hill out of the mist.

Edward commanded the center of his line, flanked by Lord Hastings on the left and Gloucester on the right. Clarence was with Edward, probably so the king could keep his eye on his unreliable brother. Warwick's divisions were led by Montagu in the center, Oxford on the right, and Exeter on the left. Warwick, with his reserve troops, directed all three divisions from the rear.

The battle quickly became confused. As Edward had moved forward during the night, the armies became overlapped. As the fighting began Oxford and Gloucester found no one facing them. While Edward's division battled those of Montagu and Exeter, Oxford was able to outflank Hastings and attack him from the side. Hastings's men broke ranks and ran back through Barnet, with Oxford's soldiers in pursuit. When Warwick learned this, he sent a messenger to ask Oxford to gather his forces and rejoin the battle.

Meanwhile Gloucester, to the right of Edward, had the same opportunity. He led his division around a ravine and attacked Exeter from the side. Warwick sent some of his reinforcements to Exeter and forced Gloucester to retreat. Edward, seeing Gloucester in trouble, sent some of his troops to help his brother. In the dense fog he had no way of knowing that his left wing, under Hastings, had crumbled. Hastings, however, had managed to regroup some of his soldiers and was threatening Montagu.

Confusion at Barnet

In all the confusion the line of battle had turned. Instead of stretching east to west, the two armies now battled one another across a line running north to south. As Montagu's soldiers battled hand to hand with Hastings's, they were suddenly attacked from the side. Oxford had gathered his men and, in response to Warwick's message, came galloping back, intending to attack Edward from behind. In the fog he could not tell that the battle line had shifted.

Because of the fog Montagu's men thought that the banners bearing Oxford's symbol—a glowing star—displayed Edward's symbol—the bright sun he had adopted after seeing the triple suns before the Battle of Mortimer's Cross. They turned to meet this new enemy, and their archers poured volley after volley into the oncoming troops. Oxford's army, however, could recognize that it was Montagu's soldiers firing on it. A cry of "Treason! Treason!" went up. Oxford, thinking the Nevilles had changed sides in the middle of the battle, fled from the scene, taking all his troops. How ironic it was that, after

On April 14, 1471, the Lancastrians battled the Yorkists near the village of Barnet. As the battle lines shifted in the dense fog, confused Lancastrian soldiers began attacking their own forces.

Richard Neville, earl of Warwick, is slain at the Battle of Barnet by Yorkist soldiers.

all the battles of the Wars of the Roses decided by treachery, this one was decided by an accident thought to be treachery.

The battle had now lasted three hours. Exeter was dead. Montagu was killed shortly afterward. One story said that he had withdrawn his men, preparing to go over to Edward's side, and that Warwick learned of his plan and sent his own men to kill his brother.

The Death of the Kingmaker

Warwick tried to rally what remained of his forces, but his soldiers began to throw aside their weapons and run for their lives. Finally Warwick did the same. He usually fought on horseback, but Montagu had convinced him to set a good example to

his men by fighting on foot with them. Now, he ran back to where the horses had been tied, hoping to flee and fight another day. It was not to be. Slowed by his heavy armor, Richard Neville, earl of Warwick, was caught by Yorkist soldiers, thrown to the ground, and stabbed to death.

On the same day that saw the end of the Kingmaker, Margaret and her son, Edward, now eighteen years old, finally reached England, landing in Weymouth in the far southwest. Within a few days Oxford joined her, as did Somerset, who had escaped the slaughter at Barnet. Margaret was devastated by their news of King Edward's victory and Warwick's death: "When she heard all this miserable chances, so suddenly, one in another's neck [coming one after another]," one chronicle said, "she . . . fell to the ground, her heart was pierced with sorrow, her

The Death of Prince Edward

Most accounts of the Battle of Tewkesbury say that Queen Margaret's son, Prince Edward, was killed on the field of battle. Edward Hall, in his Union of the Two Noble and Illustre Famelies of Lancastre and York, *published in 1542, had a different version. It is found in* English Historical Documents, *edited by A. R. Myers.*

"The queen was found [after the battle] in her chariot almost dead for sorrow, the prince was apprehended and kept close by Sir Richard Crofts. . . . After the field [battle] was ended, King Edward made a proclamation that whosoever could bring Prince Edward to him alive or dead should have an annuity of £100 during his life, and the prince's life would be saved. Sir Richard Crofts, a wise and valiant knight, not at all mistrusting the king's former promise, brought forth his prisoner Prince Edward, being a goodly girlish looking and well-featured young gentleman. When King Edward had viewed him well, he asked him how he durst [dared] so presumptuously enter his realm with his banner displayed. The prince, being bold of stomach and of a good courage, answered saying, 'To recover my father's kingdom and heritage, from his father and grandfather to him, and from him, after him, to me lineally descended.' At which words King Edward said nothing, but with his hand thrust him from him (or, as some say, struck him with his gauntlet [armored glove]) whom at once they that stood about, which were George, Duke of Clarence, Richard, Duke of Gloucester, Thomas, Marquis of Dorset, and William, Lord Hastings, suddenly murdered and pitifully slew. The bitterness of which murder some of the actors [participants] afterwards in their latter days [tested] and assayed [analyzed] by the very rod of justice and punishment of God. His body was interred in homely fashion."

speech was in a manner gone, all her spirits were tormented with melancholy."[56]

Some of her advisers urged her to return to France. Others said that she should ride north to join forces with Jasper Tudor, who was forming an army in Wales. Together, they said, they could de-feat Edward, who had lost many men at Barnet. Margaret, always a fighter, chose to march toward Wales. Along the way she showed herself and her son to the people, urging them to join her. Many did.

King Edward, after the Battle of Barnet, returned to London to publicly display the corpses of Montagu and Warwick and put Henry VI back in the Tower of London. When Edward learned of Margaret's landing and destination, he hurried westward to intercept her. He knew that her strength, combined with Jasper Tudor's, might be too strong for him.

Margaret and Somerset hoped to reach Wales by crossing the Severn River at Gloucester but after a long, hard march, found the city gates closed against them. They were forced to continue north, knowing that Edward, with his usual speed, was not far behind. Their next goal was the bridge at the town of Tewkesbury. With Margaret urging them on, the weary Lancastrian soldiers reached Tewkesbury about 5 P.M. and could go no farther. They camped for the night and awaited the battle they knew would come the next morning.

Edward's army, likewise, had been pushing itself to the limit. It had come so far so fast that "his people might not find, in all the way, horse-meat, nor man's-meat, nor so much as drink for their horses, save in one little brook, where was full little relief."[57] When his scouts reported that Margaret's army had camped, Edward also stopped about three miles away.

The Battle of Tewkesbury

The next morning, May 4, Somerset drew his troops into a line of battle on a ridge south of Tewkesbury. He commanded the right wing; Prince Edward, assisted by Lord Wenlock, the center; and the earl of Devon, the left. Edward took command of his central division, with Gloucester on his left and Hastings on his right. The ground over

which Edward would have to charge was "so evil lanes, and deep dykes [ditches], so many hedges, trees, and bushes, that it was right hard to approach [the enemy] near."[58] Before the battle began, Edward sent a force of two hundred spearmen around his left flank, which was hidden from the Lancastrians by a hill.

The battle opened with Gloucester's division opening fire with arrows and cannons against Somerset's troops. For some unexplained reason, Somerset gave up his defensive position and moved down from the ridge to attack Gloucester. Perhaps he thought the trees and hedges would conceal his movement and he could surprise Gloucester. The result was that Edward's hidden spearmen, seeing an opportunity, rushed forward and fell on Somerset from behind. Caught between two forces, Somerset's division was quickly broken.

Somerset managed to escape and make his way back to the central division. He confronted Lord Wenlock and accused him of treason for not coming to his aid. After a brief, bitter argument, Somerset raised his battle ax and crushed Wenlock's skull.

The Lancastrians, seeing their leaders killing one another, knew the battle was lost. Many were chased by the victorious Yorkists into the river, where they sank under the weight of their armor and drowned. Others ran into the town and frantically banged on doors, seeking to hide.

Margaret managed to hide in a house, but her son was not so lucky. Prince Edward was dead. Most accounts say he was killed as the Lancastrian lines began to collapse and that he called out to Clarence to save him. Another story said that he was captured and brought before

Edward, then killed by Clarence and Gloucester.

Others, including Somerset, took refuge in Tewkesbury Abbey, claiming sanctuary. King Edward, seemingly always in a forgiving mood after a victory, allowed them to stay. Gloucester, however, was not so forgiving. Two days after the battle he had Somerset and the rest dragged from the abbey, and they were beheaded in the marketplace.

Margaret's Will Broken

Edward's victory would soon be complete. Margaret was found and captured. When she was told that her son was dead, her seemingly unbreakable spirit finally was shattered. When Edward returned to London, she was taken with him, riding silently in a cart.

Edward needed to return to London quickly. Another army, led by the illegitimate son of Warwick's uncle, Lord Fauconberg, had landed in southeast England and marched on London, hoping to rescue Henry VI. The Londoners stoutly resisted him, however, and when he learned about Edward's victory at Tewkesbury, he withdrew and later surrendered.

Edward entered London on May 21. That night, a final chapter was written to the story of the house of Lancaster. Henry VI, who had become king as an infant and who had never learned how to rule, was put to death. How he was killed, or by whom, remains a mystery.

The remainder of the reign of Edward IV was years of peace and prosperity such as England had not known for decades. Edward had his fill of war and glory. In-

The Yorkists emerged victorious from the Battle of Tewkesbury on May 4, 1471. As a result of the conflict, Prince Edward, the last Lancastrian claimant to the throne, was dead.

stead, he wanted to make England, and himself, rich. He promoted trade with the rest of Europe. He sought learning in addition to wealth and was a patron of William Caxton, the printer who translated many classical works into English.

As always, he continued to lead a life of pleasure. He ate enormous meals and drank great quantities of wine. Warwick once said that he would rather fight fifty battles for Edward than eat one dinner with him. He loved the company of women and had love affairs almost without number. He once joked that he always maintained "three concubines [mistresses] which in diverse proportion diversely excelled, one the merriest, the other the wiliest, the third the holiest harlot in the realm."[59]

Edward went to war only once more. He agreed to an alliance with Burgundy to attack France. Raising a large sum of money from Parliament and from benevolences (forced gifts or loans), he equipped a huge army—larger than any of Edward III or Henry V—and sailed to Calais on July 4, 1475. He was disgusted to find that the duke of Burgundy, who had been supposed to meet him there, was off fighting in Germany.

A Poor Showing

As King Edward IV advanced on London before the Battle of Barnet, the earl of Warwick's brother, the archbishop of York, tried to rally the Londoners to resist him. One of his strategies was to bring the dimwitted Henry VI before the public in a procession. What happened is told in The Great Chronicle of London *and is found in J. R. Lander's* The Wars of the Roses.

"Then at London by the means of Sir Thomas Cook and few other was means of provision made to keep King Edward out of the city which by this time drew fast thitherward. And for to cause the citizens to bear their more favour unto King Henry, the said King Henry was conveyed from the palace of Paul's through Cheap and Cornhill, and so about to his said lodging again by Candlewick Street and Watling Street, being accompanied with the archbishop of York which held him all that way by the hand and the Lord Zouche, an old and impotent man, which that day being Sheer Thursday about nine of the clock, bare [carried] the king's sword, and so with a small company of gentlemen going on foot before, and one being on horseback and bearing a pole or long shaft with two fox tails [a symbol of defiance] fastened upon the said shaft's end, held with a small company of serving men following, the progress before shewed, the which was more like a play than the showing of a prince to win men's hearts, for by this mean he lost many and won none or right few, and ever he was shewed in a long blue gown of velvet as though he had no moo [more] to change with [to wear]. But ere this progress was fully finished King Edward's fore riders were comen to Shoreditch and Newington, wherefore the said archbishop having small confidence in the citizens that they would resist King Edward or his people, shifted for himself and left King Henry in the palace as alone."

King Louis XI of France took advantage of the situation to make peace with Edward. The two kings met at Picquigny on the Somme River in France. The meeting place was on a bridge across the river. Edward and Louis agreed to a nine-year truce. Edward's oldest daughter, Elizabeth, was to marry Louis's son. Edward was to remove his army from France in return for a huge cash payment. The final part of the deal was that Louis would pay Edward fifty thousand gold crowns to buy the freedom of Margaret of Anjou, who had been living under guard in England. She would die in 1482 in Anjou. Her final years were spent mostly alone and in virtual poverty.

Louis XI (pictured) made peace with Edward IV in 1475. The two kings agreed to a nine-year truce which allied France and England.

Family Squabbles

Edward's only real problems came from within his own family. His brother, Clarence, had married Warwick's daughter, Isobel, and Clarence thought all the dead earl's estates would come to him. But Edward's other brother, Gloucester, had set his sights on marrying Warwick's younger daughter Anne, now the widow of Prince Edward. After the Battle of Tewkesbury, Anne had gone into hiding, working in London as a kitchen maid. Gloucester found her and asked Edward for permission to marry her. The king agreed, much to Clarence's dismay.

Edward continued to place more and more trust in Gloucester, who had always been loyal to him. He made his brother the virtual ruler of northern England. Gloucester proved to be a popular leader, well liked by the people, and a good soldier, fighting off attacks from Scotland.

Clarence, meanwhile, was once more feeling left out. He could not understand why Edward did not trust him, even though he had a history of betrayal. When his wife died in 1476, he wanted to wed Mary, only child of the duke of Burgundy. Edward did not trust Clarence enough to allow him to be in a position to become the duke of Burgundy. He forbade the marriage. Clarence now "seemed gradually to withdraw himself from the king's presence, hardly ever to utter a word in council, and not without reluctance to eat and drink in the king's abode."[60]

Finally, when Clarence was discovered to have been behind two minor rebellions and to have executed one of his late wife's servants without any kind of trial, Edward had had enough. In 1478 he summoned

Meeting of the Kings

A peace agreement between England and France was reached in 1475 when Edward IV and Louis XI met on a bridge over the Somme River at Picquigny in France. Philippe de Commynes, a Burgundian observer, described the meeting of the monarchs. His account is found in The Wars of the Roses *by J. R. Lander.*

"The king of England advanced along the causeway . . . very nobly attended, with the air and presence of a king: there were in his train his brother the duke of Clarence, the earl of Northumberland, his chamberlain the Lord Hastings, his chancellor, and other peers of the realm; among whom there were not above three or four dressed in cloth of gold like himself. The king of England wore a black velvet cap upon his head, with a large fleur de lys [flower design] made of precious stones upon it: he was a prince of a noble and majestic presence, but a little inclining to corpulence [fat]. I had seen him before when the earl of Warwick drove him out of his kingdom; then I thought him much handsomer, and to the best of my rememberance, my eyes had never beheld a more handsome person. When he came within a little distance of the barrier [a screen erected in the middle of the bridge], he pulled off his cap, and bowed himself within half a foot of the ground; and the king of France, who was then leaning against the barrier, received him with abundance of reverence and respect. They embraced through the holes of the grate, and the king of England making him another low bow, the king of France saluted him thus: 'Cousin, you are heartily welcome; there is no person living I was so ambitious of seeing, and God be thanked that this interview is upon so good an occasion.' The king of England returned the compliment in very good French."

Clarence before him, had him arrested for "committing acts violating the laws of the realm," and sent him as a prisoner to the Tower of London.[61] When Parliament put the duke on trial, the outcome was never in doubt. No one would go against Edward's wishes. As one writer of the time put it, "No one argued against the Duke except the King, and no one answered the King except the Duke."[62]

Clarence was sentenced to death, but Edward hesitated to have the sentence carried out, possibly out of concern for their mother, who still lived. At last, as so often happened during the Wars of the Roses, death came after dark and in secret. On

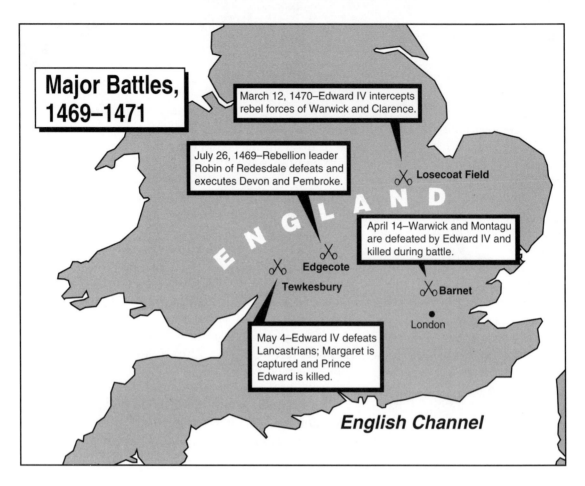

Major Battles,
1469–1471

March 12, 1470–Edward IV intercepts rebel forces of Warwick and Clarence.

July 26, 1469–Rebellion leader Robin of Redesdale defeats and executes Devon and Pembroke.

Losecoat Field

E N G L A N D

April 14–Warwick and Montagu are defeated by Edward IV and killed during battle.

Edgecote

Tewkesbury

Barnet

London

May 4–Edward IV defeats Lancastrians; Margaret is captured and Prince Edward is killed.

English Channel

February 18, 1479, Clarence was put to death in the Tower. Tradition says that at his own request he was drowned in a butt, or large barrel, of his favorite wine.

Edward's Death

By 1482, although he was only forty, Edward's health began to fail. A lifetime of luxurious living had taken its toll. His once magnificent body had become "marvellous gross."[63] He died on April 9, 1483, probably of appendicitis. While on his deathbed he placed his heir, his twelve-year-old son, Prince Edward, in the care of his brother, Gloucester.

Edward's exploits had led to triumph for the house of York. His premature death would be its downfall. Once more England had a boy king, and the struggle for power around him would usher in the last phase of the Wars of the Roses.

Chapter

6 The Princes in the Tower

When Edward IV died in 1483, he left as his heir his twelve-year-old son, Edward. As usual in England, however, the boy king was the object of a fight for power. Edward V would never be crowned and would reign less than half a year. His fate, and that of his younger brother, would become one of the great mysteries of the Wars of the Roses—a mystery still unsolved.

The young Edward had been born in 1470 while his mother, Queen Elizabeth, was in sanctuary in Westminster Abbey after Warwick and Clarence had forced Edward IV to flee England. Most of his childhood was spent in the company of his mother's family, the Woodvilles, and his governor was Lord Rivers, Elizabeth's brother. Long before the death of Edward IV, the Woodvilles were looking ahead to their positions under his son's reign. They made sure that those closest to the prince, and on whom he depended the most, were members of their family. Sir Thomas More, who wrote *The History of King Richard III* in the early 1500s, said, "In effect, everyone as he was nearest of kin unto the Queen, so was planted next about the prince, whereby her blood might of youth be rooted in the Prince's favour."[64]

When his father died, Prince Edward was at Ludlow Castle, his home on the Welsh border. The queen and her younger son, Richard, duke of York, who had been born in 1473, were in London. The Woodvilles had expected the queen to be protector in case Edward IV died

Following Edward V's succession to the English monarchy in 1483, the young king became the object of a ruthless power struggle.

before his son was old enough to rule on his own. In fact, Edward IV had said so in his will that was made in 1475.

It must have come as a shock, therefore, when Edward IV, on his deathbed, named Richard of Gloucester as protector. Perhaps Edward thought his brother would be a more trustworthy guardian for his son than the Woodvilles, who had a reputation for greed. And in an age filled with treachery, Gloucester had always remained loyal to Edward.

Gloucester was far away in northern England, at his castle at Middleham, when his brother died. The Woodvilles took advantage of his absence to try to secure their position. First, a messenger was sent to Ludlow, telling Rivers to bring the young king to London as quickly as possible. Then the royal council, dominated by Elizabeth's relatives, set May 4—less than a month after Edward IV's death—as the date for Edward V's coronation. The early date was chosen because Gloucester's role as protector would cease once Edward was crowned. The Woodvilles also took control of the royal treasure, dividing it among Elizabeth, Thomas Grey (marquess of Dorset and Elizabeth's son by her first marriage), and her brother Edward Woodville. Dorset was deputy constable of the Tower of London, and Edward commander of the royal navy.

On his deathbed, Edward IV named his brother Richard of Gloucester (pictured) protector of young Edward V. His role as guardian would cease once Edward was formally crowned.

Gloucester Warned

One member of the council, Lord Hastings, was a friend of Gloucester's and hated the Woodvilles, supposedly because of a quarrel with Dorset over Elizabeth Shore, one of the late king's mistresses. Hastings sent an urgent message to Gloucester, advising him of the Woodvilles' plans and urging him to try to intercept the young king before he arrived in London.

Gloucester received Hastings's message on about April 17 and immediately headed south. He sent messages to some of the northern nobles loyal to him to meet him in York on April 20. Meanwhile, Rivers had not responded as quickly to his message from London. It was not until April 23 that he left Ludlow with King Edward.

When Gloucester reached the city of Nottingham, a message reached him from Henry Stafford, duke of Buckingham, who had heard of Edward IV's death and offered his services to Gloucester. They agreed to meet at Northampton and take control of the young king. Each of them wrote to Edward "to ascertain from him on what day and by what route he intended to enter the capital, so they could join him, that in their company his entry to the City might be more magnificent."[65] They also wrote to Rivers, asking him to wait for them in Northampton.

When the two dukes reached Northampton on April 29, however, they found

The Struggle for Control

After the death of King Edward IV in 1483, a struggle for control of the new king, twelve-year-old Edward V, broke out between Queen Elizabeth and her family on one hand and the king's uncle, Richard of Gloucester, on the other. Italian observer Dominic Mancini described the early stages of this conflict. It is contained in The Wars of the Roses *by J. R. Lander.*

"On completion of the royal obsequies [funeral] . . . a council assembled before the arrival of the young King Edward and Richard duke of Gloucester. . . . Two opinions were propounded [offered]. One was that the duke of Gloucester should govern, because Edward in his will had so directed, and because by law the government ought to devolve on [be given to] him. But this was the losing resolution; the winning was that the government should be carried on by many persons among whom the duke, so far from being excluded, should be accounted the chief. . . . All who favoured the queen's family voted for this proposal, as they were afraid that, if Richard took unto himself the crown or even governed alone, they, who bore the blame for Clarence's death, would suffer death or at least be ejected from their high estate. According to common report, the chamberlain Hastings reported all these deliberations by letter and messengers to the duke of Gloucester, because he had a friendship of long standing with the duke and was hostile to the entire kin of the queen on account of the marquess [Queen Elizabeth's son by her first marriage]. Besides, it was reported that he advised the duke to hasten to the capital with a strong force and avenge the insult done him by his enemies. He might easily obtain his revenge if, before reaching the city, he took the young King Edward under his protection and authority, while seizing before they were alive [alert] to the danger those of the king's followers, who were not in agreement with this policy."

that Rivers and the king had left that morning and traveled fourteen miles south to Stony Stratford. Rivers had been met by Sir Richard Grey, Queen Elizabeth's other son from her first marriage, who urged him to come to London without delay. Rather than remaining with the king, however, Rivers and Grey rode back to Northampton to meet Gloucester and Buckingham, leaving orders to proceed toward London the next morning with or without them.

When they reached Northampton, Rivers and Grey found Gloucester and Buckingham in a friendly mood. They all had a jolly dinner with plenty of wine before Rivers and Grey went to bed. Gloucester and Buckingham, however, sat up far into the night making their plans. When Rivers awoke the next morning, he was trapped. Gloucester and Buckingham had surrounded the inn with their soldiers. Gloucester confronted Rivers, accusing him of trying to keep the king from the protector named by his father. Leaving Rivers under guard but taking Grey with them, Gloucester and Buckingham set out for Stony Stratford.

The Respectful Uncle

When they arrived, King Edward had not yet left. Gloucester greeted his nephew respectfully, paying "every mark of respect to the King his nephew, in the way of uncovering his head, bending the knee."[66] He told Edward that the Woodvilles had, by encouraging Edward IV's rich lifestyle, hastened his death. He said that he, Gloucester, was more capable of helping Edward rule than these "puny men."[67]

When Grey tried to interrupt, Gloucester had him arrested, along with some of Edward's closest Woodville attendants.

Gloucester now had Edward in his power. When the news reached London, there was panic among the Woodvilles. Queen Elizabeth once more took refuge in Westminster Abbey, along with all her daughters and Prince Richard. When the archbishop of York visited her, More wrote, he found "much heaviness, rumble, haste and business, carriage and conveyance of her stuff into sanctuary—chests, coffers [strongboxes], packs, fardelles [bundles], trusses [bound bundles], all on men's backs . . . some going, some discharging [unloading], some coming for more, some breaking down the walls."[68]

After forcing his nephew from the protection of Lord Rivers and Sir Richard Grey, Richard of Gloucester assumed the role as protector of Edward V.

Gloucester and his nephew arrived in London on May 4, the date originally scheduled for Edward's coronation. Edward was at first housed in the bishop of London's palace, but at a council meeting on May 10, Buckingham suggested that the bishop's palace was too shabby and that Edward should be moved to the Tower of London. No one thought this was at all threatening. The Tower, begun by William the Conqueror in 1066 and added onto many times since, had traditionally been the residence of English kings before their coronations. True, it had also been used as a prison, but not primarily, as it would in later centuries.

The council also formally named Gloucester protector, "with the consent and goodwill of the lords, with power to order and forbid in every matter, just like another king."[69] A new date, June 22, was set for Edward's coronation. Gloucester also tried to get the council to condemn Rivers and Grey, but the council was unwilling to go this far. He also tried to convince Queen Elizabeth to emerge from Westminster Abbey with the children, but she refused.

The Downfall of Hastings

Gloucester must have known that Edward, once he came of age, would favor the Woodvilles. It was probably at about this time, although no one knows for certain, that he decided to take the throne from his nephew instead of ruling the kingdom through him. To do so he began to eliminate those opposed to him. On June 11 he sent Richard Ratcliffe, a member of his staff, northward with orders to have

Rivers, Grey, and others who had been arrested at Stony Stratford put to death.

It was not enough, however, to eliminate the Woodvilles. Gloucester also feared opposition from those whose loyalty was to Edward IV and his sons. This included Lord Hastings, who was now uneasy about Gloucester's plans. At a meeting of the council on June 13, Gloucester suddenly asked Hastings what punishment was deserved by those "who conspire against the life of one so nearly related to the king as myself, and entrusted with the government of the realm?"

Confused, Hastings replied, "Certainly if they have done so heinously [wickedly] they are worth a heinous punishment."

"What!" shouted Gloucester. "Dost thou serve me with 'ifs' and 'ands'? I tell thee they [the Woodvilles] have done it, and that I will make good upon thy body, traitor!"[70]

With that, Gloucester shouted "Treason!" and banged his fist loudly on the table. This was his signal for armed men who had been waiting outside to rush in and arrest Hastings and the other members of the council whom Gloucester suspected. Hastings was hauled outside and hardly given time to say his prayers before his head was forced down on a piece of timber and hacked off.

With Hastings dead, no one on the council dared oppose Gloucester's wishes. Historian Polydore Vergil, writing in the next century, said that "Men began to look for nothing else than cruel slaughter, as perceived they well that Duke Richard would spare no man so that he might obtain the kingdom."[71] Another chronicle said that many people supported Gloucester "rather for fear than any hope of benefit."[72]

One important person, the king's younger brother, remained outside

Gloucester's control. In a council meeting on June 16, Gloucester "submitted how improper it seemed that the King should be crowned in the absence of his brother, who, on account of his nearness of kin and his station [position as duke of York], ought to play an important part in the ceremony."[73] The council, now in fear of Gloucester, agreed that soldiers should be sent to Westminster Abbey and Queen Elizabeth ordered to give up her youngest son.

That same day Gloucester "came with a great multitude to Westminster . . . armed with swords and staves [staffs]."[74] Before forcing his way into the sanctuary, however, he sent the duke of Norfolk, one of his strongest supporters, and the archbishop of Canterbury to try to get Elizabeth to give up young Prince Richard voluntarily. They appealed to her to let the nine-year-old boy join his brother, who they said was lonely living in the Tower. Elizabeth knew the boy would probably be taken from her by force if she did not give in, so yielded, "trusting in the word of the Cardinal [archbishop] of Canterbury that the boy should be restored [returned] after the coronation."[75]

In order to usurp the English throne, Richard of Gloucester sequestered Edward V and his younger brother in the Tower of London.

"Loving Words"

The young Richard was conveyed to Westminster Palace, "my Lord Protector [Gloucester] receiving him at the Star Chamber door with many loving words."[76] From there he was taken by boat down the Thames River to the Tower of London. Now he and his brother were both in the ancient fortress, from which neither would emerge alive.

Next, Gloucester convinced the council to postpone Edward's coronation. No one knows what excuse he used. Then on Sunday, June 22, the day on which the coronation was to have taken place, Gloucester made his intentions public. He had several submissive ministers preach in their sermons that Edward was not the true king because his father, Edward IV, "was conceived in adultery, and in every way was unlike the late duke of York; but Richard, duke of Gloucester, who altogether resembled his father, was to come to the throne as the legitimate successor."[77]

The people of London were unconvinced. They had approved Gloucester's actions in removing the king from his Woodville relatives, but they had turned against him when he had the popular Hastings killed. Furthermore, they knew

---

Richard Springs a Trap

After his father's death young Edward V was escorted to London by Lord Rivers and the marquess of Dorset, Queen Elizabeth's brother and son. At Northampton they were met by Richard, duke of Gloucester, who appeared so friendly that Rivers decided to stay the night with him there, while Edward stayed a few miles down the road in Stony Stratford. Sir Thomas More, in his History of King Richard III, *tells what happened next. The passage is found in J. R. Lander's* The Wars of the Roses.

"Now was the king in his way to London gone from Northampton, when these dukes of Gloucester and Buckingham came thither. Where remained behind the Lord Ryvers, the king's uncle, intending on the morrow to follow the king and be with him at Stony Stratford [fourteen] miles hence, early ere he departed. So was there made that night much friendly cheer between these dukes and the Lord Ryvers a great while. But [immediately] after that they were openly with great courtesy departed and the Lord Ryvers lodged, the dukes secretly with a few of their most privy [intimate] friends set them down in council, wherein they spent a great part of the night. And at their rising in the dawning of the day, they [Gloucester and Buckingham] sent about privily [secretly] to their servants in their inns and lodging about, giving them commandment to make themselves shortly ready. . . . Upon which messages, many of their folk were attendant when many of the Lord Ryvers' servants were unready. Now had these two dukes taken also into their custody the keys of the inn, that none should pass forth without their license. And over [in addition to] this, in the highway towards Stony Stratford, where the king lay, they had bestowed certain of their folk that should send back again and compel to return any man that were got out of Northampton towards Stony Stratford. . . . But when the Lord Ryvers understood the gates closed and the ways on every side beset, neither his servants nor himself suffered [allowed] to go out, perceiving well so great a thing without his knowledge not begun for naught, comparing this manner present with this last night's cheer, in so few hours so great a change marvelously misliked."

that an army summoned by Gloucester from his northern estates was on its way to London and were afraid of being ruled by military force.

Gloucester tried another strategy. On June 8 a bishop named Stillington had come before the council claiming that Edward IV's marriage to Elizabeth Woodville was invalid. The late king, he said, had previously entered into a contract to marry Lady Eleanor Butler. Stillington said that he personally had presided at a ceremony that, according to the law of the time, was not a marriage but was just as legally binding. The bishop said that he and Lady Eleanor, who had died in 1468, had remained silent because they feared the Woodvilles. Furthermore, Stillington produced "instruments [legal documents], authentic doctors, proctors and notaries of the law with depositions [testimonies] of divers witnesses" to prove his story.[78]

If Stillington's story was true, Edward IV had not been legally free to marry Elizabeth Woodville, and their children, indeed, were illegitimate. There is no evidence today that the contract story was true, but none of the writers at the time claimed that it was false. Regardless, it was the story now put forth by Gloucester. On June 23 Buckingham, now Gloucester's chief ally, spoke to the lord mayor and leading citizens in London's Guildhall— something like a city hall. He said that, on the basis of Edward IV's contract with Lady Eleanor, Gloucester was the rightful king.

False Enthusiasm

His appeal was met with silence from the Londoners. Finally, according to Thomas More, some of Buckingham's men stationed throughout the crowd began to toss their caps in the air and shout, "King Richard! King Richard!" Two days later Buckingham spoke again, this time to a large assembly of both nobles and commoners at Westminster. He read a petition, urging Gloucester to accept the crown. The people listened and

> consulted their own safety, warned by the example of Hastings and perceiving the alliance of the two Dukes [Gloucester and Buckingham], whose power supported by a multitude of troops, would be difficult and hazardous to resist; and therefore they determined to declare Richard their king and ask him to undertake the burden of office.[79]

On June 26 Buckingham led a delegation to Gloucester's residence, Baynard's Castle. There he implored Gloucester to accept the throne. Gloucester, in More's version, at first pretended to be reluctant but when Buckingham renewed his plea, finally agreed. He immediately rode to Westminster Palace and, like his brother before him, took his seat on the throne.

Many of the preparations that had been made for Edward V's coronation now were put to use by his uncle. On July 6 Richard of Gloucester was crowned King Richard III in a magnificent ceremony at Westminster Abbey. Beside him was his queen, Warwick's daughter Anne. Their son, seven-year-old Edward, had been left at Middleham. The former queen, Elizabeth Woodville, remained in sanctuary in another part of the abbey.

But where were the former king, Edward V, and his younger brother, Richard, duke of York? This question, no

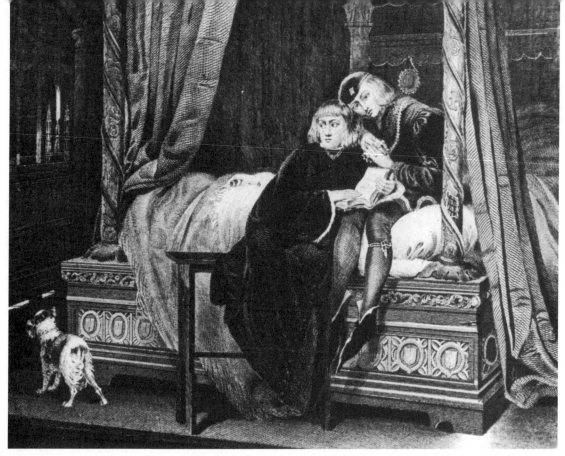

Mystery continues to shroud the fate of Edward V and Richard, duke of York. The princes are believed to have met their deaths within the Tower of London.

doubt whispered to one another by the people of England at the time, has puzzled historians ever since. The fate of the two boys, who have come to be known as the princes in the Tower, is the greatest mystery of the Wars of the Roses. There is little doubt that they were murdered, but when and by whom? No one knows for certain. As Audrey Williamson wrote in her book about the princes, "In fact the rumors of the methods used to murder the two princes are so various and so conflicting that the tales positively emphasize the only certainty: that no one knew or knows how they died, or even if and when they did."[80]

The Princes Disappear

At first after young Richard was taken to the Tower to join his brother, the two boys had some degree of freedom. *The Great Chronicle of London* records that "During this Mayor's year [1482–1483], the children of King Edward were seen shooting and playing in the garden of the Tower by sundry [various] times."[81] Italian Dominic Mancini wrote that soon the princes were "withdrawn to the inner apartments of the Tower proper, and day by day began to be seen more rarely behind the bars and windows."[82]

The Fall of Hastings

Lord Hastings had been one of Edward IV's closest friends. Although he also supported Richard of Gloucester, Gloucester was afraid Hastings might stand in the way of his claiming the throne in place of Edward's son. How Gloucester did away with him is described in this passage from The Great Chronicle of London *found in* A. R. Myers's Historical English Documents.

"And in all this season the Lord Hastings was had in great favour with the said protector [Gloucester] and received of him many great benefits and gifts, as many other noble men did, and all to bring his evil purpose about. And thus driving and delaying the time till he had compassed [made up] his mind, upon the 13th day of June [1483] he appointed a council to be held within the Tower, to the which were invited the Earl of Derby, the Lord Hastings with many others, but most of such as he knew would favour his cause. And upon the same day dined the said Lord Hastings with him and after dinner rode behind him or behind the Duke of Buckingham to the Tower, where when they with the other lords were entered into the council chamber, and communed for a while of such matters as he had previously proposed, suddenly one made an outcry at the said council chamber door, 'Treason, treason!' and forthwith the usher opened the door and then pressed in such men as were before appointed and straightway laid hands upon the Earl of Derby and the Lord Hastings; and at once without any process of law or lawful examination led the said Lord Hastings out unto the green beside the chapel and there, upon an end of squared piece of timber, without any long confession or other space of repentance, struck off his head. And thus was this noble man murdered for his truth and fidelity which he firmly bare [bore] unto his master [Edward IV], upon whose souls and those of all Christians may Jesus have mercy, Amen!"

Mancini, who left England shortly before Richard's coronation, wrote that "already there was a suspicion that he [Edward V] had been done away with."[83] Yet *The Croyland Chronicle* states that after the coronation, while Richard made a tour of the kingdom, "King Edward IV's two sons were in the Tower of London under special guard."[84]

Late in July while Richard was still on his tour, Elizabeth Woodville and her brothers were involved in a plot to sneak her daughters out of Westminster Abbey and across the English Channel to France.

Spies discovered what has come to be known as the Sanctuary Plot, however, and reported it to Richard, who increased security around Westminster Abbey so that it "assumed the appearance of a castle and fortress, while men of the greatest austerity [sternness] were appointed by King Richard to act as the keepers thereof."[85] The plot failed, but it may have convinced Richard that he would never be secure as long as Edward IV's sons lived.

Of the many versions of what happened to the princes in the Tower, the one most accepted was written by Thomas More in about 1515. More was able to interview people who had been part of the events of 1483 to 1485 and were in the best position to know what had happened. It was More's version that was used by Shakespeare in his play *Richard III*.

According to More, King Richard, who was in Gloucester when he learned of the Sanctuary Plot, was so alarmed that he sent one of his men, John Green, to London. He was to go to the Tower and give its constable, Sir Robert Brackenbury, "a letter and credence [credentials] that the same Sir Robert should in any wise put the two children to death."[86] Brackenbury, however, refused to carry out the order.

Green returned to Richard, who was then at Warwick, and reported his failure. According to More, Richard said, "Ah, whom shall a man trust?" A page answered, "Sir, there lieth one on your pallet without that I dare well say to do your Grace pleasure the thing were right hard that he would refuse."[87] The page referred to Sir James Tyrell, who had been in Richard's service for ten years and had seen others receive greater rewards.

Richard moved on to York and from there, records prove, sent Tyrell to London on August 30 to collect some robes to be used at a ceremony making Richard's son, Edward, Prince of Wales. With Tyrell went his horse keeper, John Dighton. More wrote that Tyrell took with him a letter from Richard instructing Brackenbury to surrender all the keys of the Tower for one night.

Death in the Night

Tyrell, More's story goes, received the keys from Brackenbury and that night, approximately September 3, went to the boys' cell and remained outside while Dighton and a man named Miles Forest, "a fellow fleshed in murder," smothered the two boys with their feather bed and pillows.[88] Then, after showing the bodies to Tyrell,

According to Thomas More (pictured), a reputable scholar and writer, the princes in the Tower were smothered by order of King Richard III.

Dighton and Forest buried them at the foot of a staircase.

Many other versions of the princes' death have been written. They describe the brothers as having been killed with a sword, buried alive, drowned in wine, or sealed in a room to starve to death. Some writers claim they were killed by Buckingham instead of Richard. Others say they remained prisoners until the reign of Richard's successor, Henry VII, who had them killed.

The Deaths of the Princes

The most famous version of how the two young sons of Edward IV met their deaths was written by Sir Thomas More. This is the version used by William Shakespeare in his play Richard III. *It is quoted in J. R. Lander's* The Wars of the Roses.

"But forthwith was the prince and his brother both shut up: and all others removed from them, only one called Black Will or William Slaughter except, set to serve them and see them sure [safe]. After which time the prince never tied his points [shoelaces], nor aught wraught of himself [had any thought], but with that young babe his brother lingered in thought and heaviness till this traitorous death delivered them of that wretchedness. For Sir James Tyrell devised that they should be murdered in their beds. To the execution whereof, he appointed Miles Forest, one of the four that kept them, a fellow fleshed in murder beforetime. To him he joined one John Dighton, his own horsekeeper, a big broad, square, strong knave. Then, all the others being removed from them, this Miles Forest and John Dighton, about midnight (the silly [innocent] children lying in their beds) came into the chamber and suddenly lapped them up among the clothes, so bewrapped them and entangled them, keeping down by force the feather bed and pillows hard unto their mouths, that within a while, smothered and stifled, their breath failing, they gave up to God their innocent souls into the joys of heaven, leaving to the tormentors their bodies dead in the bed. Which after that the wretches perceived, first by the struggling with the pains of death, and after long lying still, to be thoroughly dead: they laid their bodies naked out upon the bed, and fetched Sir James to see them. Which, upon the sight of them, caused those murderers to bury them at the stair foot, meetly deep in the ground, under a great heap of stones."

Tyrell was suspected of the murders even before his supposed confession and long before More was writing.

White Tower

The other event that seemed to verify More's story occurred in 1674 when workmen in the Tower of London uncovered a wooden chest at the foot of a staircase in the White Tower. Inside were the skeletons of two children. Most people assumed these were the remains of Edward V and his brother. The bones were placed in an urn and buried in Westminster Abbey. In 1933 they were dug up and examined by medical experts, who determined that they belonged to children of about the same ages as the princes. Other experts have since attempted to cast doubt on this, but no one has been able to prove that the skeletons were not those of Edward IV's sons. In her book on the subject, Alison Weir wrote, "No other pair of boys of rank disappeared in the Tower between 1483 and 1674: to suggest otherwise is really to stretch coincidence too far."[90]

It must have seemed during the final years of the reign of Edward IV that the house of York was firmly settled on the throne of England. The house of Lancaster was all but extinct. Perhaps the only thing that could have changed matters would have been for the house of York to turn against itself. That is exactly what had happened. Richard III had become king, but his methods had so appalled his subjects that the stage was set for another invasion, one that would finally end the Wars of the Roses.

In 1674 a wooden chest was unearthed in the White Tower (pictured). Inside were the skeletons of two children, believed to be the remains of the young princes.

More's version seems the most believable. For one thing, he claimed to have gotten the details from Tyrell's confession, made in 1502 while he was under arrest in the Tower. No record of such a confession exists, but More, a reputable scholar, claimed to have seen it. Tyrell was never charged with the princes' murders but was beheaded in 1502 for treason against Henry VII.

The Great Chronicle of London said, "But howsoever they [the princes] were put to death, certain it was before that day [Easter 1484] they were departed this world, of which cruel deed Sir James Tyrell was reported to be the doer."[89] This passage, written before 1502, shows that

7 Bosworth

If Thomas More's account is true, the two young sons of Edward IV were dead in September 1483. Richard III, however, was far from secure. He was unpopular, especially when rumors spread that the princes had been murdered. He would soon face rebellion at home from one of his strongest friends. Also, there was one last, faint hope of the house of Lancaster to deal with.

Henry Tudor, earl of Richmond, had been born in 1457. Through his mother, Margaret Beaufort, he was the great-great-grandson of John of Gaunt and the last surviving member of the house of Lancaster. In 1471, after the Battle of Tewkesbury, Henry fled from England to the French coastal area of Brittany with his uncle, Jasper, earl of Pembroke. The following year Edward IV attempted to convince the duke of Brittany to return Henry to him, claiming he wanted Henry to marry his daughter Elizabeth. The duke was warned, however, that his guest probably would be killed and refused to hand him over.

Eleven years later Henry was twenty-six years old and still living in Brittany with a small group of faithful supporters of the house of Lancaster. Throughout his long exile it must have seemed impossible that he would ever be able to challenge the house of York. The seizure of the throne by Richard III, however, gave him hope. He waited to see what would happen.

Meanwhile in England Richard, still on his royal tour in October 1483, received an unwelcome surprise. The duke of Bucking-

Henry Tudor, earl of Richmond, was the great-great-grandson of John of Gaunt and the last surviving member of the house of Lancaster.

ham, who had done more than any other man to help Richard win the throne, was rebelling against him. Buckingham had been at his castle at Brecon in Wales. He had as his prisoner John Morton, bishop of Ely, one of those loyal to the memory of Edward IV who had been arrested the same day Hastings was executed.

According to More, Buckingham learned in mid-September about the murder of the princes and was sickened. Buckingham said to Morton that when he "was credibly informed of the death of the two young innocents, O Lord, how my veins panted, how my body trembled and my heart inwardly grudged [complained]."[91] Some historians believe that Buckingham told Margaret Beaufort, now married to Lord Thomas Stanley, about the princes and that she and Morton convinced him to support Margaret's son, Henry.

According to Thomas More, when the duke of Buckingham (pictured) learned of the princes' murder, he rebelled against King Richard and pledged his support to Henry Tudor.

A Plan of Action

On September 24 Buckingham sent a letter to Henry in Brittany, pledging his support for an invasion. After additional communication October 18 was selected as the date. The plan called for Henry's supporters in southern and western England to form an army and march on London, while at the same time Buckingham would advance with his troops from Wales and join Henry, who would land on the southwestern coast.

A noteworthy aspect of Buckingham's rebellion was that it supported Henry, not the young King Edward V. This would indicate that most of the people involved firmly believed that Edward and his brother were dead. Polydore Vergil wrote that Lady Margaret Stanley, Henry's mother, informed the boys' mother, Queen Elizabeth, who

> fell into a swoon and lay lifeless a good while; after coming to herself, she wept, she cried aloud, and with lamentable shrieks made all the house ring. She struck her breast, tore and cut her hair, and prayed also for her own death, calling by name her most dear children and condemning herself for a madwoman for that, being deceived by false promises, she had delivered her younger son out of sanctuary to be murdered by his enemy.[92]

Lady Margaret's plan was to make her son's claim stronger through a marriage with Elizabeth's oldest daughter, also named Elizabeth. The former queen

Believing that her sons had been murdered, Queen Elizabeth (pictured) agreed to a marriage between her oldest daughter, Elizabeth, and Henry Tudor, earl of Richmond.

Richard Reacts

Richard acted quickly. He sent word to his supporters in Wales to "pounce upon all his [Buckingham's] property" if he moved from his castle.[93] So it was that when Buckingham set out with an army on October 18, intending to cross the Severn River and join Henry, Sir Thomas Vaughan, Buckingham's neighbor, moved in and captured his castle. Even the weather worked in Richard's favor. Ten straight days of heavy rain had caused the Severn River to rise to the point where Buckingham could not cross. Unable to return to his castle and deserted by his troops, he took refuge with one of his tenants, who betrayed him to Richard's men. On November 2 he was executed in the marketplace at Salisbury.

On the same day Henry's ships were finally able to reach England. He approached the harbor city of Plymouth. Armed men went to meet him in a small boat. Claiming to be Buckingham's soldiers, they assured him all was well. Henry was suspicious and later sent spies into the city. When he learned that Buckingham's rebellion had failed, he sailed back to Brittany. Many of the rebels were executed, but Richard was lenient with Lady Margaret. He needed the support of her husband too much.

Richard returned in triumph to London on November 24, but his position was, if anything, less secure than before. Rumors about the murders of the princes were everywhere, and the people were shocked. This age was rough and violent, but the murder of defenseless children was something no one could overlook. Vergil wrote that "when the fame of this notable

agreed to the marriage and to support Henry's claim to the throne, something she would scarcely have done if she had any hope that her sons were still alive.

Nothing went as planned. Henry sailed from Brittany on October 3, but a violent storm forced his ships back to port. His supporters in Kent, southeast of London, began their revolt on October 10, a week too early. The duke of Norfolk, Richard's close ally, immediately moved south and blocked the rebels' crossing of the Thames River. Norfolk learned about Buckingham's involvement from some captured rebel leaders and sent word to the king.

foul fact was dispersed through the realm, so great grief struck literally to the heart of all men that the same, subduing all fear, wept everywhere."[94] Whether Richard had actually caused the deaths of his nephews was much less important than the fact that most people believed that he had.

Henry and his followers had by no means given up. On Christmas Day in Rennes Cathedral in Brittany, he took a

Buckingham's Rebellion

Richard III's closest ally was Henry Stafford, duke of Buckingham. Finally, however, he too turned against the king and toward Henry Tudor. Buckingham's failure and his death are described in The Croyland Chronicle, *this section of which is found in J. R. Lander's* The Wars of the Roses.

"Henry, duke of Buckingham, who at this time was living at Brecknock [Brecon] in Wales, had repented of his former conduct, and would be the chief mover in this attempt [a rebellion], while a rumour was spread that the sons of King Edward before-named had died a violent death, but it was uncertain how. . . . To him [Henry Tudor] a message was, accordingly, sent, by the duke of Buckingham . . . requesting him to hasten over to England as soon as he possibly could, for the purpose of marrying Elizabeth, the eldest daughter of the late king, and, at the same time, together with her, taking possession of the throne. The whole design of this plot, however, by means of spies, became perfectly well known to King Richard, who . . . contrived that, throughout Wales, as well as in all parts of the marches thereof, armed men should be set in readiness around the said duke [Buckingham], as soon as ever he had set a foot from his home, to pounce upon all his property. . . . Finding that he [Buckingham] was placed in a position of extreme difficulty, and that he could in no direction find a safe mode of escape, he first changed his dress, and then secretly left his people; but was at last discovered in the cottage of a poor man, in consequence of a greater quantity of provisions than usual being carried thither. Upon this, he was led to the city of Salisbury, on the day of the commemoration of All Souls [November 2]; and, notwithstanding the fact that it was the Lord's day, the duke suffered capital punishment in the public market-place of that city."

vow that if he ever became king of England, he would marry Princess Elizabeth, Edward IV's daughter. This vow raised the opinion of Henry in the minds of those nobles loyal to the house of York but opposed to Richard. In increasing numbers they promised to support him.

Parliament met for the first and only time of Richard's reign on January 24, 1484. One of its first acts was to pass an act called Titulus Regius (royal title), confirming Richard as king and declaring the marriage of Edward IV and Elizabeth Woodville invalid. Legally only a church court could have ruled on the marriage, but Parliament was too afraid of Richard to go against his wishes.

Richard's Reign

The most peaceful and productive part of Richard III's reign was in the first half of 1484. Laws were passed that gave some measure of legal aid to the poor, began a system of bail for accused criminals, reformed certain land laws, outlawed benevolences (forced loans to the king), and established qualifications for jury duty. John Rous, a chronicler of the time, who had little good to say about Richard after the king's death, wrote that during his reign Richard was "an especial good lord."[95] And in 1525 a mayor of London said, "Although the king did evil, yet in his time were many good acts made."[96]

In March Queen Elizabeth allowed her daughters to emerge from the sanctuary of Westminster Abbey. Before doing so, however, she made Richard swear publicly that he would not harm them. Richard promised

that if the daughters of Dame Elizabeth Grey, late calling herself Queen of England, will come to me out of the Sanctuary at Westminster, and be guided, ruled and demeaned [behave properly] after me, then I shall see that they be in surety of their lives, and also not suffer any manner hurt by any manner persons, nor any of them imprison within the Tower of London or any other prison.[97]

The specific reference to the Tower of London is another sign that Elizabeth knew the fate of her sons and blamed it on Richard.

Richard's happiness was to end shortly. On April 9 his only son, Edward, died at Middleham Castle. Although the boy had always been in poor health, Richard and Queen Anne took his death hard. "You might have seen his father and mother in a state almost bordering upon madness by reason of their sudden grief," one chronicler wrote.[98] Many people saw the death as Richard's punishment from God for the princes' murders. More wrote, "Many Englishmen declared that the imprecations [curses] of the agonised mother [Elizabeth] had been heard."[99]

Sorrow and Scandal

More personal sorrow lay ahead for Richard, as well as a scandal. His queen, Anne, had been ill for some time, and the death of her son seemed to make her worse. By Christmas it was apparent to observers that Anne was dying. It also appeared that a new queen was on the horizon—Edward IV's eighteen-year-old daughter, Elizabeth.

Elizabeth (pictured), daughter of Edward IV and Elizabeth Woodville, emerged from Westminster Abbey in 1484. The young princess was courted by both Henry Tudor and Richard III.

Sometime during the summer of 1484, Elizabeth's mother had finally been convinced to emerge from Westminster Abbey. At Christmas, *The Croyland Chronicle* says, "the lady Elizabeth was, with her four younger sisters, sent by her mother to attend the Queen [Anne] at court." Elizabeth was very beautiful and attracted Richard's attention. *The Croyland Chronicle* continued:

> The fact ought not to be concealed that, during this feast of the Nativity, far too much attention was given to dancing and gaiety, and vain changes of apparel presented to Queen Anne and the Lady Elizabeth, the eldest

daughter of the late king, being of similar colour and shape; a thing that caused the people to murmur and the nobles and prelates greatly to wonder thereat; while it was said by many that the king was bent, either on the anticipated death of the queen taking place, or else, by means of a divorce, for which he supposed he had quite sufficient grounds, on contracting a marriage with the said Elizabeth.[100]

No one knows exactly what kind of attraction, if any, there was between Richard and his lovely niece. He never had been known as a womanizer, as was his brother Edward. It may have been that a marriage with Elizabeth would solve two political problems. First, he could have another son to inherit the throne after him. Second, marrying Elizabeth would keep her from marrying Henry.

It may have been, also, that Elizabeth and her mother were attracted by the idea of the marriage. Even though it is likely that the former queen believed Richard to be the murderer of her two sons, she had always sought power. This would be a chance to make her daughter queen and restore the fortunes of the Woodvilles.

Evil Rumors

Anne died on March 16, 1485. By this time people were willing to believe anything evil about Richard. One record of the time said there was "much simple communication among the people, by evil-disposed persons, showing how that the Queen, as by consent and will of the King, was poisoned, for and to the intent

A Poetic Complaint

As the reign of Richard III continued, more and more people grew hostile to him. His loss of support among the common people of London was reflected in an unflattering rhyme about him and his advisers, as described in The Great Chronicle of London *found in* The Wars of the Roses *by J. R. Lander.*

"In these days were chief rulers about the king, the Lord Lovell, and two gentlemen being named Mr. Ratclyff and Mr. Catesby. Of the which persons was made a seditious [rebellious] rhyme and fastened upon the Cross in Cheap and other places of the city whereof the sentence was a followeth, 'The cat, the rat, and Lovell our dog, rulen all England, under an hog.' This was to mean that the forenamed three persons as the Lord Lovell and the other two that is to mean Catesby and Ratclyff ruled this land under the king which bare [carried] a white boar for his cognizance [his personal symbol]. For the devisers of this rhyme much search was made and sundry [some] accused to their charges, but finally two gentlemen named Turberville and Collingbourne were for that and other things laid to charge, arrested and cast in prison, for whom shortly after as upon the [date missing from manuscript] was holden at the Guildhall an oyer and terminer [trial] where the said two gentlemen were arraigned, and that one of them called Collingbourne convicted of that crime and other. For the which upon the [date missing from manuscript] following he [Collingbourne] was drawn unto the Tower Hill and there full cruelly put to death, at first hanged and straight cut down and ripped, and his bowels cast into a fire. The which torment was so speedily done that when the butcher pulled out his heart he spake and said JHESUS JHESUS. This man was greatly monyd [admired] of the people for his goodly personage and favour of visage [appearance]."

that he might then marry and have to wife Lady Elizabeth."[101] People also whispered that Richard and Elizabeth had been lovers months before Anne's death. Writing in the 1600s, George Buck said he had seen a letter written by Elizabeth early in 1485 saying that "she was his in heart and in thought, in body and in all."[102]

The country refused to condone even the idea of such a marriage. Richard's closest advisers, Richard Ratcliffe and William Catesby, advised him that if he did not abandon his intended purpose and deny it by public declaration, all the people of the north, in whom he placed the greatest trust, would rise in rebellion and impute [attribute] to him the death of the Queen, through whom he had first gained his present high position, in order that he might gratify his incestuous passion of his niece, something abominable before God.[103]

Richard took their advice and at a large public gathering "showed his grief and displeasure and said it never came in his thought or mind to marry in such manner-wise."[104]

This rejection by Richard did not please Elizabeth. According to a poem written shortly afterward, she was convinced by her mother and by Lady Margaret to join the forces supporting Henry. The poem says that Elizabeth sent a ring to Henry, pledging to marry him if he won the crown. Richard may have discovered Elizabeth's betrayal. Sometime in the spring he sent her away from court and housed her in a castle in remote Yorkshire.

Preparing for Invasion

Rumors about an invasion began to fill the air. More nobles every day were quietly abandoning Richard and crossing the channel to Henry. As early as the previous Christmas "news was brought to [Richard] from his spies beyond the sea that, notwithstanding the potency and splendour of his royal estate, his adversaries would, without question, invade the kingdom during the following summer."[105]

In the summer of 1485 Richard made an attempt to capture Henry. He offered the duke of Brittany a bribe to hand his guest over. Just at this time the duke became ill, and his treasurer, thinking to make a profit for himself, agreed to surrender Henry. Henry was warned of the plan and escaped, exchanging clothes with a servant and crossing the border into France in disguise.

As an invasion became increasingly certain, more and more nobles either wrote to Henry, pledging to support him, or crossed over to France to join him. One important addition for Henry was John de Vere, earl of Oxford, who would become Henry's most experienced commander.

While in exile, Henry Tudor (pictured) planned to invade the kingdom and overthrow Richard III. Nobles increasingly offered their support as discontent with the king escalated.

By midsummer Richard was preparing for the invasion. He issued commissions of array, which called on men for military service, in every county. He ignored his own laws against forced loans to raise money to pay troops. He wrote to all nobles loyal to him to maintain a lookout along every coast. He knew Henry was coming but did not know where. The king assembled his army at Nottingham, in the center of the kingdom, so he would be ready to march in any direction.

Henry sailed on August 1 from the French port of Harfleur. His force was small, only about two thousand men. He would have to rely on more troops to join him after he landed in England. He came ashore August 7 at Milford Haven on the southwestern coast of Wales. This made good sense. The Tudors were a Welsh family, and Henry could depend on the Welsh to rally to him.

Richard's chief lieutenant in Wales was Rhys ap Thomas. Thomas had vowed that no rebels would go through Wales "except they should pass over his belly," meaning unless he was killed.[106] According to one story Thomas went over to Henry's side but kept his vow by first standing under a bridge while Henry walked over.

Henry made his way through Wales, picking up more troops as he went. Richard's communications were so poor that he did not learn of Henry's landing until August 12. He was furious to learn that his enemy had come as far east as Shrewsbury without being opposed.

Fearing a Lancastrian overthrow, King Richard (pictured) assembled an army of nearly ten thousand men to prevent Henry Tudor's invasion.

Richard's Suspicions

The man who should have stopped Henry's advance was Sir William Stanley. The Stanleys had been among Richard's major supporters, but the king was beginning to suspect their loyalty. After all, Sir William's brother, Lord Thomas Stanley, was married to Henry's mother, Margaret. Richard ordered Lord Stanley to come to him, but Stanley claimed to be ill. Richard then arrested Stanley's son, vowing to kill the young man if his father joined the rebels.

Richard had managed to raise a large army—about ten thousand men. His chief commanders were John Howard, duke of Norfolk, and Henry Percy, earl of Northumberland. The army marched west to meet Henry. On August 21 it left the city of Leicester and camped that night near

The Case Against Richard III

During the reign of King Henry VII, his predecessor, Richard III, was portrayed as one of the blackest, most monstrous villains that ever walked the earth. This summary of Richard's misdeeds was written by John Rous in 1491. It is found in A. R. Myers's English Historical Documents.

"And in short he [Richard III] imprisoned King Edward V, king in deed but not crowned, with his brother Richard, taken from Westminster under promise of safety, so that it was afterwards known to very few by what death they were martyred. Then he ascended the throne of the dead princes, whose protector he had been in their minority, this tyrant King Richard, who was born at Fotheringhay in the county of Northampton, retained for two years in his mother's womb and issuing forth with teeth and hair down to his shoulders. . . . At his birth Scorpio was in the ascendant, whose sign is the house of Mars. And as Scorpio was smooth in countenance but deadly with his tail, so Richard showed himself. He received this lord King Edward V blandly with embraces and kisses, and yet within about three months or little more he had killed him with his brother, and he poisoned the lady Anne, his queen, daughter of the Earl of Warwick. He imprisoned during his lifetime his mother-in-law Anne, the dowager countess, lady and just heir of that noble lordship [Warwick]. . . . And what was most detestable to God and to all the English, indeed to all nations who shall hear of it, he killed that most holy man king Henry VI, either by others or, as many believe, by his own hands."

the small town of Market Bosworth. Henry's army, about half the size of Richard's, was about three miles away.

Moving toward both forces were about three thousand Stanley troops, commanded by Sir William. They had been summoned by Richard. Lord Thomas Stanley, however, had been in communication with Henry. Henry tried to convince him to desert the king and join him. Stanley refused to commit one way or the other. He told Henry only that he would "come to him with his army well appointed."[107] Stanley was going to see how things developed before taking sides.

On the next day, August 22, 1485, Richard arranged his army on the crest of Ambien Hill south of Market Bosworth. At the front was a body of archers, commanded by Norfolk. Richard was just behind with the foot soldiers. At the rear, at his own request, was Northumberland.

Henry arranged his own outnumbered army, "trusting to the aid of Thomas Stanley," and advanced up the hill.[108] Once Henry passed a marsh on his right, Richard gave the order to attack, telling his troops, "Everyone give but one sure stroke and the day is ours. What prevaileth a handful of men to a whole realm? As for me, I assure you this day I will triumph by glorious victory or suffer death for immortal fame."[109]

The Battle of Bosworth

Henry's front line was made up of archers commanded by Oxford. They opened fire on Norfolk's troops but could not force them to abandon their position on the hill. Oxford then charged up the hill and engaged the enemy in hand-to-hand fighting "thus hot on both sides."[110] Norfolk was killed, but Oxford still could not make his way up the hill. Northumberland should have come forward to help but did not. At the last minute he had decided to stay out of the fight. Once more treachery would decide a battle.

Richard decided to risk everything on one bold move. If he could reach Henry and kill him, he thought, his enemies would lose heart and surrender. With a small escort the king charged from Ambien Hill and headed straight for Henry. Richard himself killed Henry's standard-bearer and knocked the powerful Sir John Cheney off his horse. The men around Henry wavered, but at that moment Sir William Stanley decided to enter the battle on Henry's side. Richard was prevented from reaching Henry. His horse was killed, and Catesby advised him to flee. In a fa-

mous speech from Shakespeare's *Richard III*, the king refused, shouting:

> Slave! I have set my life upon a cast,
> And I will stand the hazard of the die.
> I think there be six Richmonds
> [Henry Tudors] in the field;
> Five have I slain today, instead of
> him.—
> A horse! A horse! My kingdom for a
> horse![111]

At last, however, Richard was surrounded, and "alone was killed fighting manfully in the thickest press of his enemies."[112]

With the death of King Richard III, the Battle of Bosworth quickly came to an

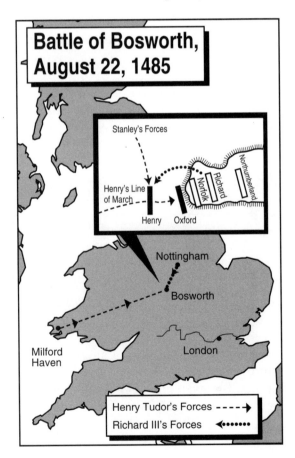

Battle of Bosworth, August 22, 1485

Stanley's Forces

Henry's Line of March

Henry   Oxford   Norfolk   Richard   Northumberland

Nottingham

Bosworth

Milford Haven

London

Henry Tudor's Forces ----→
Richard III's Forces ◄••••••

(Left) Richard III bravely charges toward Henry Tudor during the Battle of Bosworth. (Below) In the end, the triumphant Henry would be crowned Henry VII, king of England.

end. Oxford was finally able to overcome the remainder of Norfolk's troops. Elsewhere the slain king's men began to run for their lives. Others "forthwith threw away weapon and freely submitted themselves to Henry's obedience."[113]

Richard had worn a crown on top of his helmet. After the battle the crown was found by Lord Stanley and brought to Henry. There, on the battlefield, Stanley "set anon King Richard's crown . . . upon his head, as though he had been already by commandment of the people proclaimed king after the manner of his ancestors."[114]

The body of the former king was treated with disrespect; it was stripped naked, thrown across a horse, and carried back to Leicester. On the way his head was bruised when it was knocked against a stone bridge. At Leicester, two days later, Richard III was buried "without any pomp or solemn funeral."[115]

The Wars of the Roses had ended after thirty years of bloodshed and slaughter. Henry would take the throne as Henry VII. He would later marry Elizabeth of York, and the houses of Lancaster and York, such bitter enemies for so many years, would be joined in the new house of Tudor.

Calm After the Storm

The Wars of the Roses were much like a storm at sea. On top, wind howls and waves crash, while beneath the surface all is calm. During the Wars of the Roses, the great majority of English subjects were hardly affected at all, while the highest level of society suffered great upheaval. A foreigner observed:

> England enjoyed this peculiar mercy above all other kingdoms, that neither the country nor the people, nor the houses were wasted, destroyed or demolished; but the calamities and misfortunes of war fell only upon the soldiers, and especially upon the nobility.[116]

Some of the noblest families of England, those that had wielded enormous power for many generations, were wiped out, including the Nevilles, the Beauforts, and even the ruling Plantagenets. Many other families, while not wiped out, had their most able leaders killed in battle, executed, or banished. Historian George M. Trevelyan wrote that the Wars of the Roses were "a bleeding operation performed by the nobility upon their own body."[117]

New noble families took the places of the old, but they were different in character. The old nobility had included several ancient families that, over time, had consolidated their estates until they were al-most as powerful as the kings. The newer nobility owed everything to the kings who gave them their titles. By 1509 only two of the great families—the Staffords, the dukes of Buckingham, and the Percys, the earls of Northumberland—remained with their estates intact.

The nobility thus lost much of its wealth and influence. The great lords of

The nobility of England was dramatically affected by the Wars of the Roses. Some of the noblest, most powerful families in England were completely wiped out.

England were no longer in a position to dictate to the king, as had happened many times before, including Richard II and the Lords Appellant. This change did not mean England would be free from revolution, but future revolutions would be by the middle class as represented by Parliament. As Charles Ross wrote: "The disappearance of the higher nobility as rivals to the royal authority, and of their capacity to disrupt normal political life by force, marks a momentous change in the character of English politics."[118]

A Stronger Monarchy

The nobility's loss of power was the monarchy's gain. Henry VII had learned a valuable lesson. He had lived through a time when mighty subjects repeatedly challenged kings. He was determined that it would not happen to him. "The way was thus prepared," Trevelyan wrote, "for the Tudor policy of bridling [restraining] 'overmighty subjects.'"[119] Under the Tudors the monarchy became more powerful and wealthy than ever before.

Henry VII and his descendants were aided in becoming powerful and wealthy by the middle class—the merchants, traders, and small landowners who had taken almost no active part in the Wars of the Roses. These people wanted, above everything else, peace and stability. England had had enough of the storms of war and revolution. The Wars of the Roses made the country ready for the strong rule of the Tudors. "An increase in the power

The nobility's loss of power was a boon to the monarchy. During the reign of Henry VII (pictured) the monarchy increased its power and wealth, while England experienced domestic peace and stability.

of the crown," wrote Ross, "was considered a small price to pay for domestic peace."[120]

This domestic peace would last, with few exceptions, for more than 150 years. During that time the Renaissance, the rebirth of learning and culture that began in Italy about 1400, would at last find its way to England, having been delayed by the Hundred Years' War and Wars of the Roses. Under the granddaughter of Henry Tudor and Elizabeth of York, Queen Elizabeth I, the country would undergo a blossoming of art, music, and literature. It would take its place among the leading nations of Europe and begin to lay the foundations of the British Empire.

Notes

Introduction: A Family Affair

1. S. B. Chimes, quoted in A. L. Rowse, *Bosworth Field: From Medieval to Tudor England.* Garden City, NY: Doubleday, 1966.

2. Charles Ross, *The Wars of the Roses: A Concise History.* London: Thames and Hudson, 1992.

3. Quoted in Ross, *The Wars of the Roses.*

4. C. W. C. Oman, quoted in J. R. Lander, *The Wars of the Roses.* New York: G. P. Putnam's Sons, 1966.

Chapter 1: The House of Lancaster

5. Rowse, *Bosworth Field.*

6. Quoted in Rowse, *Bosworth Field.*

7. Adam of Usk, *Chronicon Adae de Usk (Chronicle of Adam of Usk).* Translated by Edward Maunde Thompson. London: Henry Frowde, 1904.

8. Jean de Froissart, *Froissart's Chronicles.* Translated by John Jolliffe. New York: Modern Library, 1967.

9. Quoted in Thomas B. Costain, *The Last Plantagenets.* Garden City, NY: Doubleday, 1962.

10. Quoted in Lander, *The Wars of the Roses.*

11. Ross, *The Wars of the Roses.*

12. Quoted in Franklin Hamilton, *Challenge for a Throne: The Wars of the Roses.* New York: Dial Press, 1967.

13. Hamilton, *Challenge for a Throne.*

14. Quoted in Hamilton, *Challenge for a Throne.*

Chapter 2: The Duke and the Queen

15. T. F. Tout, quoted in Rowse, *Bosworth Field.*

16. Quoted in Hamilton, *Challenge for a Throne.*

17. Quoted in Hamilton, *Challenge for a Throne.*

18. Quoted in Hamilton, *Challenge for a Throne.*

19. Quoted in Paul Murray Kendall, *Warwick the Kingmaker.* New York: W. W. Norton, 1987.

20. Quoted in Hamilton, *Challenge for a Throne.*

21. Quoted in Lander, *The Wars of the Roses.*

22. Quoted in Rowse, *Bosworth Field.*

23. Quoted in Hamilton, *Challenge for a Throne.*

24. *An English Chronicle of the Reigns of Richard II, Henry IV, Henry V, and Henry VI,* quoted in Lander, *The Wars of the Roses.*

25. Quoted in Kendall, *Warwick the Kingmaker.*

26. Quoted in Kendall, *Warwick the Kingmaker.*

27. Quoted in Rowse, *Bosworth Field.*

28. Quoted in Rowse, *Bosworth Field.*

29. Philippe Erlanger, *Margaret of Anjou: Queen of England.* Coral Gables, FL: University of Miami Press, 1971.

Chapter 3: "This Sun of York"

30. Ross, *The Wars of the Roses.*

31. Quoted in Rowse, *Bosworth Field.*

32. Kendall, *Warwick the Kingmaker.*

33. Ross, *The Wars of the Roses.*

34. Quoted in Hamilton, *Challenge for a Throne.*

35. *Richard III,* act 1, scene 1. *The Living Shakespeare,* edited by Oscar James Campbell. New York: Macmillan, 1958.

36. Quoted in Hamilton, *Challenge for a Throne*.

37. Quoted in Hamilton, *Challenge for a Throne*.

38. Quoted in Eric N. Simons, *The Reign of Edward IV*. New York: Barnes and Noble, 1966.

Chapter 4: The Kingmaker

39. Quoted in Simons, *The Reign of Edward IV*.
40. Ross, *The Wars of the Roses*.
41. Quoted in Simons, *The Reign of Edward IV*.
42. Quoted in Hamilton, *Challenge for a Throne*.
43. Quoted in Hamilton, *Challenge for a Throne*.
44. Quoted in Simons, *The Reign of Edward IV*.
45. Quoted in Rowse, *Bosworth Field*.
46. Quoted in Hamilton, *Challenge for a Throne*.
47. *Warkworth Chronicle*, quoted in Lander, *The Wars of the Roses*.
48. Philippe de Commynes, quoted in Lander, *The Wars of the Roses*.
49. Quoted in Simons, *The Reign of Edward IV*.

Chapter 5: The Last of the Lancasters

50. Philippe de Commynes, quoted in Hamilton, *Challenge for a Throne*.
51. Quoted in Simons, *The Reign of Edward IV*.
52. Quoted in Simons, *The Reign of Edward IV*.
53. Rowse, *Bosworth Field*.
54. Quoted in Simons, *The Reign of Edward IV*.
55. Quoted in Hamilton, *Challenge for a Throne*.
56. Quoted in Simons, *The Reign of Edward IV*.
57. Quoted in Simons, *The Reign of Edward IV*.
58. Quoted in Hamilton, *Challenge for a Throne*.
59. Quoted in Rowse, *Bosworth Field*.
60. Quoted in Hamilton, *Challenge for a Throne*.

61. Quoted in Hamilton, *Challenge for a Throne*.
62. Quoted in Rowse, *Bosworth Field*.
63. Philippe de Commynes, quoted in Hamilton, *Challenge for a Throne*.

Chapter 6: The Princes in the Tower

64. Quoted in Alison Weir, *The Princes in the Tower*. New York: Ballantine, 1992.
65. Dominic Mancini, quoted in Weir, *The Princes in the Tower*.
66. Sir Thomas More, quoted in Weir, *The Princes in the Tower*.
67. Mancini, quoted in Weir, *The Princes in the Tower*.
68. Quoted in Audrey Williamson, *The Mystery of the Princes*. Chicago: Academy Chicago Publishers, 1992.
69. *The Croyland Chronicle*, quoted in Weir, *The Princes in the Tower*.
70. More, quoted in Hamilton, *Challenge for a Throne*.
71. Quoted in Weir, *The Princes in the Tower*.
72. *The Croyland Chronicle*, quoted in Weir, *The Princes in the Tower*.
73. Mancini, quoted in Weir, *The Princes in the Tower*.
74. *The Croyland Chronicle*, quoted in Weir, *The Princes in the Tower*.
75. Mancini, quoted in Weir, *The Princes in the Tower*.
76. Simon Stallworthe, quoted in Weir, *The Princes in the Tower*.
77. Mancini, quoted in Weir, *The Princes in the Tower*.
78. Philippe de Commynes, quoted in Weir, *The Princes in the Tower*.
79. Mancini, quoted in Weir, *The Princes in the Tower*.
80. Williamson, *The Mystery of the Princes*.
81. Quoted in Weir, *The Princes in the Tower*.

82. Quoted in Weir, *The Princes in the Tower.*

83. Quoted in Lander, *The Wars of the Roses.*

84. Quoted in Weir, *The Princes in the Tower.*

85. *The Croyland Chronicle*, quoted in Weir, *The Princes in the Tower.*

86. Quoted in Lander, *The Wars of the Roses.*

87. Quoted in Lander, *The Wars of the Roses.*

88. Quoted in Lander, *The Wars of the Roses.*

89. Quoted in Weir, *The Princes in the Tower.*

90. Weir, *The Princes in the Tower.*

Chapter 7: Bosworth

91. Quoted in Weir, *The Princes in the Tower.*

92. Quoted in Weir, *The Princes in the Tower.*

93. *The Croyland Chronicle*, quoted in Rowse, *Bosworth Field.*

94. Quoted in Weir, *The Princes in the Tower.*

95. Quoted in Weir, *The Princes in the Tower.*

96. Quoted in Weir, *The Princes in the Tower.*

97. Quoted in Paul Murray Kendall, *Richard the Third.* New York: W. W. Norton, 1956.

98. *The Croyland Chronicle*, quoted in Rowse, *Bosworth Field.*

99. Quoted in Weir, *The Princes in the Tower.*

100. Quoted in Lander, *The Wars of the Roses.*

101. *Acts of Court of the Mercers Company*, quoted in Weir, *The Princes in the Tower.*

102. Quoted in Weir, *The Princes in the Tower.*

103. *The Croyland Chronicle*, quoted in Rowse, *Bosworth Field.*

104. *Acts of Court of the Mercers Company*, quoted in Weir, *The Princes in the Tower.*

105. *The Croyland Chronicle*, quoted in Weir, *The Princes in the Tower.*

106. Quoted in Hamilton, *Challenge for a Throne.*

107. Vergil, quoted in Lander, *The Wars of the Roses.*

108. Vergil, quoted in Rowse, *Bosworth Field.*

109. Quoted in Hamilton, *Challenge for a Throne.*

110. Vergil, quoted in Lander, *The Wars of the Roses.*

111. *Richard III*, act 5, scene 4.

112. Vergil, quoted in Lander, *The Wars of the Roses.*

113. James Gairdner, quoted in Rowse, *Bosworth Field.*

114. Vergil, quoted in Lander, *The Wars of the Roses.*

115. Vergil, quoted in Lander, *The Wars of the Roses.*

Epilogue: Calm After the Storm

116. Philippe de Commynes, quoted in Lander, *The Wars of the Roses.*

117. George M. Trevelyan, *A Shortened History of England.* Harmondsworth, England: Penguin Books, 1962.

118. Ross, *The Wars of the Roses.*

119. Trevelyan, *A Shortened History of England.*

120. Ross, *The Wars of the Roses.*

For Further Reading

Clifford Lindsey Alderman, *Blood Red the Roses*. New York: Julian Messner, 1971. Highly readable account of the Wars of the Roses. Short on pictures, but includes bibliography, index, and suggestions for further reading.

Richard W. Barber, *England in the Middle Ages*. New York: Seabury Press, 1976. Good overview of both the political and social history of England during the Middle Ages.

Janice Young Brooks, *Kings and Queens: The Plantagenets of England*. Nashville: Thomas Nelson, 1975. A lively telling of the lives and times of the Plantagenets. Roughly half the book deals with the rulers during the Wars of the Roses.

Michael Byam, *Arms and Armor*. New York: Alfred A. Knopf, 1988. Traces the development of armor and weapons through the ages and includes the dramatic changes in armor due to both the development of the longbow and firearms.

John D. Clare, ed., *Knights in Armor*. San Diego: Harcourt Brace Jovanovich, 1992. Well-illustrated account of what knighthood meant in terms of training, armor, duties, and responsibilities.

Madeline Jones, *Knights and Castles*. London: B. T. Batsford Ltd., 1991. Part of the *How It Was* series. Excellent description of knighthood, including training, weapons, method of warfare, and castles. Also deals with the decline of the knight due to the perfection of firearms.

Gladys Malvern, *The Queen's Lady*. Philadelphia: Macrae Smith, 1963. Highly romantic fictional story of young Joanna, an attendant of Anne Neville, Richard III's queen.

Robert Louis Stevenson, *Black Arrow*. New York: St. Martin's Press, 1965. Action-packed novel about the exploits of a young knight set loosely against the background of the Wars of the Roses.

Marguerite Vance, *Song for a Lute*. New York: E. P. Dutton, 1958. Highly fictionalized biography of Anne Neville. Almost ignores deaths of Edward IV's sons.

Jan Westcott, *Set Her on a Throne*. Boston: Little, Brown, 1972. Fictional story of the life of Anne Neville, the earl of Warwick's daughter and Richard III's queen, from 1470 until her death. Highly accurate in historical details.

Sylvia Wright, *The Age of Chivalry: English Society 1200–1400*. New York: Warwick Press, 1988. Well-illustrated social and political history of England in the Middle Ages. Provides good background for the Wars of the Roses.

Works Consulted

Adam of Usk, *Chronicon Adae de Usk (Chronicle of Adam of Usk)*. Translated by Edward Maunde Thompson. London: Henry Frowde, 1904. A chronicle covering the reign of King Richard II of England, as written by a monk in his service.

Oscar James Campbell, ed., *The Living Shakespeare*. New York: Macmillan, 1958. A collection of twenty-two plays and the sonnets of Shakespeare, each accompanied by an essay detailing the history of the work.

Edward P. Cheyney, *A Shortened History of England*. Boston: Ginn, 1904. Excellent overview for the reader who wishes a short, understandable account of the basic facts.

Thomas B. Costain, *The Last Plantagenets*. Garden City, NY: Doubleday, 1962. Last of four volumes in the author's *Pageant of England* series. Reads like a novel but is soundly grounded in fact.

Philippe Erlanger, *Margaret of Anjou: Queen of England*. Coral Gables, FL: University of Miami Press, 1970. Readable, yet overly romantic, account of the life of Queen Margaret. Extensive quotations from Shakespeare, but few others.

Jean de Froissart, *Froissart's Chronicles*. Translated by John Jolliffe. New York: Modern Library, 1967. Severely abridged version of Froissart's history, although translation is readable.

Franklin Hamilton, *Challenge for a Throne: The Wars of the Roses*. New York: Dial Press, 1967. Fast-moving, highly entertaining account of the period, but lack of footnotes is a handicap to the serious student.

Michael Hicks, *Richard III: The Man Behind the Myth*. London: Collins and Brown, 1991. Attempts to ignore some of the more biased negative stories of Richard's life and reign to give a factual account concentrating on his accomplishments.

George Holmes, *The Later Middle Ages: 1272–1485*. New York: W. W. Norton, 1962. Third volume in the *Norton History of England* series. Good summary of politics and events in England; fewer details on the wars.

David Hume, *The History of England from the Invasion of Julius Caesar to the Revolution of 1688*. Boston: Little, Brown, 1854. This massive, six-volume classic of English history is now somewhat antiquated, but is a good source for facts, names, and dates.

Harold F. Hutchison, *King Henry V*. New York: Dorset Press, 1967. Thorough examination of Henry's reign and of Henry as a man. A special bonus is the appendix, the account by English soldier John Page of the siege of Rouen.

E. F. Jacob, *The Fifteenth Century: 1399–1485*. Clarendon, England: Oxford Press, 1961. Sixth volume of the *Oxford History of England* series. Goes into great detail on events in England, less on the war in France.

Paul Murray Kendall, *Richard the Third*. New York: W. W. Norton, 1956. This biography, while not ignoring the darker side of Richard's character, takes pains to show his positive traits.

————, *Warwick the Kingmaker*. New York: W. W. Norton, 1987. Well-written and balanced account of the turbulent life and times of Richard Neville, earl of Warwick. Warwick's faults are described to the same extent as his virtues.

J. R. Lander, *The Wars of the Roses*. New York: G. P. Putnam's Sons, 1966. The story of the wars and the political events surrounding them is told through the words of writers of the time—in letters, diary entries, chronicles, and legal proceedings. Lengthy passages in antiquated language can be tedious.

Elizabeth Longford, ed., *The Oxford Book of Royal Anecdotes*. Oxford, England: Oxford University Press, 1989. A superb collection of vignettes about British rulers from Roman times to the present. Most are taken from contemporary sources.

A. R. Myers, ed., *English Historical Documents: 1327–1485*. New York: Oxford University Press, 1969. The fourth in a multivolume series offering translations of all or part of documents written during the period. Includes everything from treaties to the cost of breakfast for the king's council.

Charles Ross, *The Wars of the Roses: A Concise History*. London: Thames and Hudson, 1992. Lavishly illustrated paperback version of a book that first appeared in 1976. The political, military, and social aspects of the wars are treated in different chapters, making the context hard to maintain.

A. L. Rowse, *Bosworth Field: From Medieval to Tudor England*. Garden City, NY: Doubleday, 1966. Part of the *Crossroads of World History* series. Despite the title, this is a full account of events from the overthrow of Richard II in 1399 to the early years of the reign of Henry VII.

Eric N. Simons, *The Reign of Edward IV*. New York: Barnes and Noble, 1966. Thorough and well-written story of Edward's reign. More maps and photographs would have been nice, as would have footnotes for the quotations.

George M. Trevelyan, *A Shortened History of England*. Harmondsworth, England: Penguin Books, 1962. Has been called the best single-volume history of England ever written, and with good reason. Marvelous writer gives all the whos, whens, and wheres along with the hows and whys.

Alison Weir, *The Princes in the Tower*. New York: Ballantine, 1992. This excellent account of the events surrounding the deaths of Edward IV's young sons in the Tower of London lays the blame directly at the feet of Richard III.

Audrey Williamson, *The Mystery of the Princes*. Chicago: Academy Chicago Publishers, 1992. A thorough examination of the disappearance and presumed murders of the young Edward V and duke of York. The author seeks to cast doubt on the traditional belief that the princes were murdered by their uncle, Richard III.

Index

Battle of, 36, 62
Morton, John, 85
Mowbrey, Thomas, 14

Neville, Cicely, 21
Neville, George, 39
  as archbishop of York, 47,
    51-52
  as chancellor of England,
    47
  holds Warwick in Coventry,
    61
  releases Henry VI, 56
Neville, John. *See* Montagu,
  Lord
Neville, Richard. *See*
  Salisbury, earl of
Neville, Richard. *See* Warwick,
  earl of
Nicholas of the Tower (English
  ship), 22
Norfolk, duke of, 49, 92
  Battle of Bosworth and,
    93-94
  death of, 94
  saves Battle of Towton for
    the Yorkists, 43
  warns Richard III of
    invasion, 86
Northampton, England, 32,
  73, 74
  Battle of, 32-34
Northumberland, earls of
  Henry Percy (died 1461),
    41, 43, 44
  Henry Percy, fourth earl,
    60, 92, 93-94, 96
  Ralph Percy, 46
  see also Montagu, Lord
Nottingham, England, 50, 72,
  92

Olney, England, 51
Oxford, earl of, 60, 63
  Battle of Barnet and, 61-62
  Battle of Bosworth and, 94

fights for Henry Tudor, 91

Paris, France, 58
Parliament, 14, 25, 32, 34
  of Devils, 31
Pembroke, Herbert, earl of,
  45, 50-51
Pembroke, Jasper Tudor, earl
  of, 36, 45
Philip IV (king of France), 12
Philippa (mother of Edmund
  de Mortimer), 17
Picquigny, France, 68, 69
Plantagenet dynasty, 10, 96
Plymouth, England, 55, 86
Poitiers, Battle of, 13
Pole, Michael de la. *See*
  Suffolk, duke of
Pontefract Castle, 17

Ratcliff, Richard, 90
Ravenspur, England, 16, 59
Redesdale, Robin of, 50-51
Rennes Cathedral, 87
Richard II, 13
  death of, 17
  Lords Appellant and, 14
  seizes Bolingbroke's land,
    16
  tyranny of, 15
Richard III, 80, 87, 97
  attempts to trap Henry
    Tudor, 86
  Battle of Bosworth and,
    93-94
  coronation of, 78
  courts Princess Elizabeth,
    89
    imprisons her, 91
  death of, 94
  executes Buckingham, 86
  murder of the princes and,
    81-84
Richmond, earl of. *See* Tudor
  Henry,
Rivers, Lady, 48, 49

Rivers, Lord (Anthony
    Woodville)
  as protector of Edward V,
    71-74
  death of, 75
Rivers, Lord (Richard
    Woodville), 31, 48
  as power in court of
    Edward IV, 52
  beheaded, 51
Robin of Redesdale, 50-51
Rouen, France, 58
Rous, John, 88, 93
Ruthyn, Lord Grey of, 32
Rutland, Edmund, earl of,
  21, 29, 34, 35

Saint Albans, England, 61
  First Battle of, 11, 28-29
  Second Battle of, 37
Salisbury, Richard Neville,
  beheaded, 35
  duke of York and, 33
  earl of, 27, 28, 31
  flees England, 30
  victory at Blore Heath, 29
  see also Warwick, earl of;
    York, duke of
Salisbury, England, 86, 87
Sandal Castle, 34, 60
Sandridge, England, 31, 55
Savoy, France, 48
Scales, Lord Anthony, 49
Scotland, 41, 44, 45, 46, 55
Severn River, 65, 86
Shakespeare, William
  Henry VI, 10
  Richard III, 39, 81, 82, 94
Shore, Elizabeth, 72
Shrewsbury, England, 92
Slaughter, William ("Black
  Will"), 82
Somerset, Edmund Beaufort,
  second duke of, 20, 22, 24,
    25
  arrest of, 26

Picture Credits

Cover photo: Stock Montage, Inc.

Archive Photos, 13 (bottom), 24, 36, 56, 71, 72, 81, 84

The Bettmann Archive, 10, 23, 26, 31, 34, 35, 42, 47, 49, 50, 63, 66, 68, 76, 79, 85, 89, 95 (top)

Bibliotheque Nationale, 11, 38

Library of Congress, 12, 13 (top), 14, 16, 17 (both), 18 (both), 20, 45, 97

North Wind Picture Archives, 21, 28, 32, 33, 40, 59, 60, 74, 91, 92

Stock Montage, Inc., 44, 53, 62, 86, 95 (bottom)

Reproduced in the *Photo Archive of Famous Places of the World* by Donald M. Witte, published by Dover Publications, Inc., 83

About the Author

William W. Lace is a native of Fort Worth, Texas. He holds a bachelor's degree from Texas Christian University, a master's from East Texas State University, and a doctorate from the University of North Texas. After working for newspapers in Baytown, Texas, and Fort Worth, he joined the University of Texas at Arlington as sports information director and later became the director of the news service. He is now vice chancellor for public affairs at Tarrant County Junior College in Fort Worth. He and his wife, Laura, live in Arlington and have two children. Lace's other books include biographies of baseball player Nolan Ryan, artist Michelangelo, and statesman Winston Churchill, and histories of the Hundred Years' War and Elizabethan England.